Building Blocks for Teaching Preschoolers with Special Needs

Third Edition

by

Susan R. Sandall, Ph.D.
University of Washington, Seattle

Ilene S. Schwartz, Ph.D.
University of Washington, Seattle

Gail E. Joseph, Ph.D.
University of Washington, Seattle

Ariane N. Gauvreau, Ph.D.
University of Washington, Seattle

with

Joan A. Lieber, Ph.D.
University of Maryland, College Park

Eva M. Horn, Ph.D.
University of Kansas, Lawrence

Samuel L. Odom, Ph.D.
University of North Carolina at Chapel Hill

PAUL H. BROOKES PUBLISHING CO.®

Baltimore • London • Sydney

Paul H. Brookes Publishing Co.
Post Office Box 10624
Baltimore, Maryland 21285-0624
USA

www.brookespublishing.com

Typeset by Absolute Service, Inc., Towson, Maryland.
Manufactured in the United States of America by Sheridan Books, Inc., Chelsea, Michigan

Library of Congress Cataloging-in-Publication Data

Names: Sandall, Susan Rebecka, author.
Title: Building blocks for teaching preschoolers with special needs / by Susan R. Sandall, Ph.D., University of Washington, Seattle; Ilene S. Schwartz, Ph.D., University of Washington, Seattle; Gail E. Joseph, Ph.D. University of Washington, Seattle; Ariane N. Gauvreau, Ph.D., University of Washington, Seattle; with Eva M. Horn, Ph.D., University of Kansas, Lawrence; Joan A. Lieber, Ph.D., University of Maryland, College Park; Samuel L. Odom, Ph.D., University of North Carolina at Chapel Hill.
Description: Third Edition. | Baltimore, Maryland : Paul H. Brookes Publishing Co. [2019] | Includes bibliographical references and index.
Identifiers: LCCN 2018054501 (print) | LCCN 2019004956 (ebook) | ISBN 9781681253435 (epub) | ISBN 9781681253442 (pdf) | ISBN 9781681253411 (paper)
Subjects: LCSH: Children with disabilities—Education (Preschool)—United States. | Children with social disabilities—Education (Preschool)—United States. | Inclusive education–United States. | Individualized education programs—United States.
Classification: LCC LC4019.2 (ebook) | LCC LC4019.2 .S26 2019 (print) | DDC 371.9—dc23
LC record available at https://lccn.loc.gov/2018054501

British Library Cataloguing in Publication data are available from the British Library.

2023 2022 2021 2020 2019

10 9 8 7 6 5 4 3 2 1

Contents

About the Forms

Purchasers of this book may download, print, and/or photocopy all forms in Appendix A for professional and educational use. These materials are included with the print book and are also available at www.brookespublishing.com/downloads with (case sensitive) keycode: 72ndSsA2j for both print and e-book buyers.

About the Professional Development Materials

A set of professional development modules accompanies the third edition of *Building Blocks for Teaching Preschoolers with Special Needs*. The modules may be used by faculty and other professional development providers. Suggested uses include: Sessions of a college course, part of a training workshop, or a staff meeting.

The modules align with the Building Blocks framework. The modules support and extend the main ideas and practices described in the book. The topics are as follows:

- Using the Building Blocks Framework
- Ongoing Child Assessment
- Planning for the Individual Child
- Using Visuals to Support Learning
- Applying the Building Blocks Framework to Math and Science
- Applying the Building Blocks Framework to Developmentally Appropriate Classroom Behavior
- Extending the Building Blocks Framework to Infants and Toddlers

Each module includes ready-to-use resources including the following:

- A PowerPoint slide deck
- Presenter Notes
- Learning Activities
- Helpful Resources

Users may adjust the resources to meet the needs of their audience and professional development activity.

About the Authors

Susan R. Sandall, Ph.D., Cultivate Learning, 5001 25th Avenue NE, Suite 201E, Seattle, Washington 98105

Dr. Sandall is Professor Emeritus at the University of Washington (UW). She has directed personnel preparation projects, developed curriculum materials for all age groups, and published materials on educational practices to facilitate optimal outcomes for infants, toddlers, and preschoolers with disabilities. Her scholarly interests are effective instructional practices for young children with disabilities in inclusive settings, the changing roles of teachers of young children, and effective approaches to professional development and knowledge utilization. Dr. Sandall was Principal Investigator of the National Center on Quality Teaching and Learning for the Office of Head Start; the Center continues its work as the EarlyEdU Alliance at Cultivate Learning at UW. She serves on the Division for Early Childhood (DEC) Commission on Recommended Practices and has edited publications on the practices. Dr. Sandall is on the editorial boards of *Journal of Early Intervention* and *Topics in Early Childhood Special Education.* In 2018, Dr. Sandall received an honorary doctoral degree from Stockholm University.

Ilene S. Schwartz, Ph.D., BCBA-D, Haring Center for Research and Training on Inclusive Education, Box 357925, University of Washington, Seattle, Washington 98195

Dr. Schwartz is Professor of Special Education and Director of the Haring Center at the University of Washington (UW). Dr. Schwartz is also the director of Project DATA (Developmentally Appropriate Treatment for Autism), a school-based early intervention intensive behavioral intervention program for children with autism. She has an extensive background working with young children with special needs and their families, specifically with young children with autism and related disabilities. Dr. Schwartz is the director of the Applied Behavior Analysis Program at UW and is dedicated to creating high-quality inclusive schools so that all children, regardless of their background or ability, can attend the school of their choice and receive a high-quality education. Dr. Schwartz has published numerous chapters and articles about early childhood education and social validity. She serves on the editorial review boards of *Topics in Early Childhood Special Education* and *Journal of Early Intervention.*

Gail E. Joseph, Ph.D., 322G Miller Hall, College of Education, University of Washington, Seattle, Washington 98195

Dr. Joseph is an associate professor in the area of Early Childhood and Family Studies at the University of Washington. She teaches courses, advises students, provides service, and conducts research on topics related to early care and education. Dr. Joseph has been involved in a number of research projects and training and technical assistance activities at the local, state, and national levels related to child care quality, teacher preparation, and promoting children's social-emotional development as well as preventing challenging behavior in early learning settings. She is the founding executive director of Cultivate Learning and was the principal investigator (PI) and director of the Head Start Center for Inclusion (http://Headstartinclusion.org) and co-PI of the National Center for Quality Teaching and Learning, funded by the Office of Head Start. At Cultivate Learning, Dr. Joseph oversees the work of quality ratings in all licensed child care and state prekindergarten programs in the state.

Ariane N. Gauvreau, Ph.D., 102H Miller Hall, College of Education, University of Washington, Seattle, Washington 98195

Dr. Gauvreau is a clinical faculty member and Field Director of the Special Education Program at the University of Washington. Dr. Gauvreau has extensive experience as a preschool special education teacher, home visitor, behavioral consultant, and teacher trainer and has led numerous trainings on early intervention and autism, inclusive education, promoting positive behavior support, and family-centered practices. Her research interests include effective special education teacher preparation and strategies for inclusive education. Dr. Gauvreau is principal investigator for a project exploring family-centered practices in teacher education and serves on the editorial review board of *Young Exceptional Children*.

Joan A. Lieber, Ph.D., Professor of Counseling, Higher Education, and Special Education, College of Education, Benjamin Building, University of Maryland, College Park, Maryland 20742

Dr. Lieber is a professor of special education in the College of Education at the University of Maryland (UM). Her research interests include curriculum development for young children with disabilities and those at risk for school failure. She has been in the field of early childhood special education (ECSE) for 40 years, working both in public school and university settings. Dr. Lieber has led numerous demonstration, personnel preparation, and research projects. She and colleagues from the early childhood program at UM have recently developed a blended teacher certification in early childhood education and ECSE that incorporates universal design for learning, differentiation, and individualization in each course in the program. Dr. Lieber and early childhood colleagues are also developing a curriculum for 4-year-olds in Maryland under the auspices of the Maryland State Department of Education.

Eva M. Horn, Ph.D., 1122 West Campus Drive, University of Kansas, Lawrence, Kansas 66045

Dr. Horn is a professor and investigator at the University of Kansas (KU). She has worked in early care and education, in the early childhood special education (ECSE) community, and in university settings for many years, specializing in effective strategies for supporting the development and learning of all young children. Her research focuses on designing effective curriculum and instructional strategies that maximize opportunities for all children's full participation and positive learning outcomes in natural settings, and on professional development for evidence-based early educators. She has directed numerous externally funded grants, including educator and doctoral leadership preparation and Institute of

Education Sciences research projects. She coordinates the KU early childhood education (ECE)/ECSE blended undergraduate and graduate educator and leadership preparation programs. Dr. Horn currently serves on the Division for Early Childhood (DEC) of the Council for Exceptional Children (CEC) executive board in the presidential line.

Samuel L. Odom, Ph.D., Frank Porter Graham Child Development Institute, University of North Carolina at Chapel Hill, CB-8180, 105 Smith Level Road, Chapel Hill, North Carolina 27599

Dr. Odom is the former director of the Frank Porter Graham (FPG) Child Development Institute, University of North Carolina at Chapel Hill, where he remains as a senior research scientist. He is the author or co-author of more than 175 journal articles and book chapters and has edited 10 books on early childhood intervention and developmental disabilities. His current research is addressing treatment efficacy for children and youth with autism spectrum disorder in elementary and high school grades. In addition, Dr. Odom is the co-director of the National Clearinghouse on Autism Evidence and Practice at FPG. In 2013, he received the Arnold Lucius Gesell Prize, awarded for career achievement in research on social inclusion and child development from the Theodor Hellbrugge Foundation in Munich, Germany. In 2016, Dr. Odom received an honorary doctoral degree from Stockholm University. He is currently a visiting professor at Stockholm University and San Diego State University.

Foreword

As I was preparing to write the foreword for this edition of *Building Blocks*, I reflected on what has happened in our field since 2008, when the second edition was published. Some of the notable changes or advancements in the last 10 years include

1. Continued growth in state and national investments to early care and education
2. A revised set of recommended practices in early intervention/early childhood special education (Division for Early Childhood, 2014)
3. Advancements in our knowledge base about inclusion practices, effective professional development, and other implementation supports
4. Efforts at the federal, state, and local levels to more closely align prekindergarten (pre-K) programs and standards with those in K–3

Although much has changed over the last 10 years, some things have not changed:

1. We have made almost no progress in the percentage of preschool children who are served in inclusive settings (Barton & Smith, 2015).
2. We continue to suspend/expel preschoolers not only at high rates, but we disproportionately suspend/expel young children of color and young children with disabilities.
3. Teachers continue to report training needs related to children with disabilities and children who engage in persistent challenging behavior.

Along with the continued growth and investments in early care and education, coupled with the recognition of the importance of aligning pre-K with K–3 education, has come a more explicit focus on accountability and expectations for outcomes of our early childhood programs. Over the last 5 years, there has been much attention to and debate about whether pre-K is effective in the short term and whether positive outcomes sustain over time. In many ways, pre-K is being held to a higher standard than any other single grade in our education system. Nonetheless, the future of pre-K depends on our ability to document that it is high quality, produces positive outcomes for children, and can be implemented within a variety of early care and education settings. An alarming aspect of this research on pre-K is the relative lack of attention to the effects of pre-K on children with disabilities specifically. For the readers of this book, it is not enough to produce positive outcomes for children who are typically developing; we must figure out how to support children with disabilities such that they are physically included, meaningfully engaged, and full participants in early childhood settings. We know that inclusion, when done well, has positive outcomes for children with and without disabilities.

The push for full inclusion, coupled with the focus on demonstrating the effectiveness of early education programs for all children, presents a unique challenge for educators. Significant federal resources have been spent studying the implementation of various curricula and approaches in early childhood settings and the impact of these programs on young children's outcomes. This research has been limited in the extent to which it has included the implementation and effectiveness of instructional approaches for young children with disabilities. In most evaluations of publicly funded pre-K programs, there is little or no attention given to the instructional needs of children with disabilities specifically. Implementing effective instructional approaches for children with disabilities is a complex process that requires assessment, planning, and implementation. Furthermore, teachers must do this in the context of meeting the needs of all children in the classroom. Given the breadth and depth of knowledge that is needed to implement instruction in the context of a high-quality early childhood education environment, one can better understand why systematic, individualized instruction is often not observed in early care and education settings.

I have spent most of this Foreword raising important issues facing our field. I now want to turn to how I think this text addresses many of these issues. Broadly speaking, *Building Blocks for Teaching Preschoolers with Special Needs, Third Edition,* provides a framework and strategies that can assist teachers with planning instruction for children with disabilities in the context of providing a high-quality environment for all children in the classroom. In Chapter 2, the authors address this issue directly:

> To accomplish valued or meaningful outcomes for individual children, teachers must match an individual child's goals and objectives with appropriate teaching methods and materials, decide what amount of help or assistance is needed by the child, provide this assistance, and determine whether the assistance was helpful. . . . In addition, the successful inclusion of young children is based on the assumption that the early childhood settings in which the framework will be implemented are already of high quality—places in which children are nurtured and their developmental and learning needs are met.

This text is one of the most comprehensive books available about providing instruction in early childhood classrooms. The Building Blocks framework provides a step-by-step planning process for designing high-quality learning experiences while also delivering increasingly more individualized supports to meet the needs of all children in a classroom. Although the book also includes practical strategies and ideas, those strategies and ideas are grounded in a planning process that recognizes the complexity of delivering instruction to all young children in an inclusive setting in a way that promotes engagement, participation, and inclusion. By including a framework for planning instruction, the book avoids being just a toolbox of good ideas with no understanding of how to use those ideas systematically to affect children's outcomes.

This book acknowledges and addresses the complexity of providing instruction in inclusive classrooms by clearly describing the different levels of instruction that are needed when working with children who have a range of abilities and disabilities. By doing this, the authors are proactive in addressing a common concern among teachers that much of the information they receive is not relevant for their specific context or the children with whom they work. In addition, *Building Blocks* provides information and tools on planning, implementing, and evaluating instruction. The book also provides information and guidance on issues that often are barriers to effective instruction, such as classroom management and adaptations for children with a range of special needs. In summary, it addresses all of the relevant components of instruction in a format that is useful to teachers. It provides both a framework for instruction and the information necessary for implementing instruction for all children in an inclusive setting.

Many in our field have discussed the benefits of and barriers to inclusion and what it means to include children with disabilities in a meaningful way in community-based programs. This debate has focused on the rights of children to be included and on the supports and services that are necessary for inclusion to be successful. Although the right to inclusion has become more universally accepted, as I discussed previously, we are not making much progress in terms of making inclusion a reality for many young children with disabilities.

Building Blocks represents an important step in this understanding for several reasons. First, it acknowledges the need for a variety of instructional approaches when working with children with a range of special needs. Second, it provides tools and guidance on how to decide what kind of instruction is appropriate and how to implement that instruction. Third, it puts instruction in the context of developmentally appropriate programming. In doing so, it avoids a common assumption that effective instruction and developmentally appropriate practice are somehow inconsistent with one another. Fourth and finally, this book is written in such a way that professionals from different backgrounds can use it.

Finally, the Building Blocks framework is a universal framework; that is, it is not tied to a specific theoretical or conceptual approach. On a practical level, that means it describes how instruction can be implemented in the context of a variety of different curricula or approaches. Furthermore, the authors have included information in this edition about universal design for learning and the idea that early childhood environments should be designed for the widest variety of learners possible. Building Blocks has always been about planning for *all* children, including those with disabilities and those with challenging behavior. Even though the barriers to meaningful inclusion clearly cannot be addressed in a single book, the development and use of materials such as those provided in this updated edition will have a significant impact on overcoming some of the barriers to meaningful inclusion of young children with disabilities and other special needs in community-based settings.

On a personal note, I cannot think of an author team that is more poised to write a text such as this one. I have known Drs. Sandall, Schwartz, and Joseph both personally and professionally for much of my career. I have admired them and their collaborators collectively and individually. They have a deep commitment to inclusion that shows in all aspects of their work. Their understanding of the challenges associated with implementing effective instruction in inclusive preschool settings is based on years of experience administering and teaching in programs serving young children, preparing teachers to work with young children with disabilities in inclusive settings, conducting research, and building systems of support for those educators who are doing this hard work every day. The third edition of this book reflects this experience as well as their commitment to information that is useful to those who work directly with young children and their families. One of the greatest challenges in our field is bridging the gap between research and practice. This author team knows that challenge firsthand, and they work every day to address it. *Building Blocks for Teaching Preschoolers with Special Needs, Third Edition,* reflects this unique combination of experience with and commitment to translating research into information that changes the way teachers teach and, thus, changes outcomes for children.

Mary Louise Hemmeter, Ph.D.
Vanderbilt University

REFERENCES

Barton, E. E., & Smith, B. J. (2015). Advancing high quality preschool inclusion: A discussion and recommendations from the field. *Topics in Early Childhood Special Education, 35,* 69–78.

Division for Early Childhood. (2014). *DEC recommended practices in early intervention/early childhood special education 2014.* Retrieved from http://www.dec-sped.org/recommendedpractices

Acknowledgments

What does it mean to provide specially designed instruction in an inclusive early childhood setting? What are evidence-based practices and how do they apply to young children with and without disabilities? These are questions that we were asking in 2002 when we wrote the first edition of *Building Blocks for Teaching Preschoolers with Special Needs,* and they are questions that we are still asking today. *Building Blocks* has turned out to be a user-friendly guidebook for students, teachers, practitioners, and professionals in personnel preparation who are interested in helping young children in inclusive preschool settings to succeed. We are delighted with the response *Building Blocks* has received and with the ideas and innovations that people have drawn from our work. We know, however, that our work is not done. We have witnessed dramatic change in the early learning landscape since the first and second editions, yet the teaching and learning challenges facing teachers every day in early childhood classrooms remain the same. Teachers are underpaid, programs are under-resourced, and many children arrive at the school door with even greater needs. But, the overall optimism of early childhood educators is undiminished, and we are proud of how our students and colleagues play an important role in the lives of young children. In this edition, we recognize the many inclusive early learning options in communities. We hope this new edition of *Building Blocks* is valuable and sparks even more innovation and good teaching.

Every book has many authors. Some of these authors are acknowledged publicly, and others may be unaware of the influence they have had on the text. First, we would like to thank those people who have been actively involved in the process. We have been lucky to work with a talented group of co-authors, students, and colleagues throughout the development and field-testing of *Building Blocks.* We extend our appreciation to previous authors who have moved to new stages of their lives. We welcome a new author, Ariane N. Gauvreau, who helps us extend this work.

The Building Blocks framework grew out of work that was conducted by the Early Childhood Research Institute on Inclusion (ECRII), funded by the U.S. Department of Education. As principal investigator, Samuel L. Odom assembled a multitalented group of investigators who were committed to work together despite distance and methodological boundaries in order to understand the barriers and facilitators of inclusion for young children with disabilities. We worked together for more than 5 years to collect, analyze, and make sense of a wealth of data about inclusion that parents, teachers, and children shared with us so generously.

To ensure that this study addressed the ethnic and cultural diversity of America's young children, a group of researchers in different regions of the country collaborated on its development. These researchers were affiliated with San Francisco State University, the University of Maryland, the University of North Carolina, the University of Washington, and Vanderbilt University in Nashville. The investigators included Paula Beckman, Marci Hanson, Eva M. Horn, Joan A. Lieber, Jules Marquart, and Ruth A. Wolery. We thank them for their spirit of inquiry and their collaboration.

We have also been very fortunate to have many colleagues, teachers, and mentors whose influence can easily be seen in the Building Blocks framework. These people, to whom we extend our sincere thanks, include the following:

- Diane Bricker, University of Oregon
- Mark Wolery, Vanderbilt University
- Phillip S. Strain, University of Denver, and his colleagues from his previous work at the Early Childhood Research Institute, the precursor to the ECRII, including Diane Sainato, Ohio State University; Scott McConnell, University of Minnesota; and Howard Goldstein, University of South Florida
- Judith J. Carta and her colleagues at the Juniper Garden Children's Project, University of Kansas
- Rebecca Fewell, Vanderbilt University
- Don Baer, University of Kansas
- Susan Fowler, University of Illinois
- Robert Koegel, University of California at Santa Barbara, and Glen Dunlap, University of South Florida
- Marilou Hyson and the teachers and staff at the lab school at the University of Delaware
- Our many friends and colleagues who were part of the National Center on Quality Teaching and Learning, Office of Head Start
- The innovative team at Cultivate Learning at the University of Washington
- The children, families, and teachers at the Haring Center for Research and Training in Inclusive Education at the University of Washington

We sincerely thank our friend and colleague Mary Louise Hemmeter, Vanderbilt University, for writing the forewords for all three editions. Her insights set the tone for this edition in just the right way.

Finally, a number of people helped us bring this edition to fruition. They include Matt Zabel, Angela Notari-Syverson, and Liz Wimmer at Cultivate Learning, and Heather Shrestha, Johanna Schmitter, Melissa Solarz Flanigan, Jackie Mahler, and Hudson Perigo at Paul H. Brookes Publishing Co.

SECTION I

Using the Building Blocks Framework

Building Blocks are the basis for planning for and providing individualized support and instruction for children with disabilities and other special needs within their early childhood classrooms. The framework grew out of extensive experience with teachers attempting to address the wide variety of children's learning needs within active, busy classrooms. The Building Blocks framework also grew from our experience as researchers with the Early Childhood Research Institute on Inclusion.

In this section, we describe the Building Blocks framework and provide an overview of the evidence that informs the essential components of the framework. The foundation for all children is participation in a quality early childhood program. Key ingredients for a quality early childhood program include promotion of children's active engagement, participation, and learning. Quality programs also recognize and support the importance of relationships. Quality programs create a caring environment. Nonetheless, for some children or for some of their learning needs, this quality foundation, while necessary, is not sufficient. The Building Blocks framework offers levels of support that differ in intensity and specificity to help teachers and teams address children's learning needs. For many needs, curriculum modifications and adaptations will provide appropriate levels of support. If modifications alone are not effective in helping children accomplish their learning objectives, then teachers and teams can use specially designed instruction. Such instruction can be embedded within learning opportunities that occur in typical activities and routines in the classroom, home, and community. Specially designed instruction can also occur at greater levels of intensity that we call *child-focused instruction.* Two additional components are necessary to make the framework effective. One of these components is ongoing data collection to monitor individual children's progress and to make instructional decisions. The other essential component is collaboration. Collaboration is at the heart of effective inclusive programs that ensure that engagement, participation, learning, and belonging occur for all children and their families. The first four chapters of the book give you, the reader, an understanding of the Building Blocks framework and outline the steps so that you can use the framework in your program.

Chapter 1

Introduction

Building Blocks for Teaching Preschoolers with Special Needs, Third Edition, provides examples of educational practices that support and enhance the inclusion of young children with disabilities and other special needs in community-based classrooms and early learning programs. It is designed for two primary audiences. First, teachers, caregivers, and other team members who work in community-based programs that include children with disabilities and other special needs will find the book useful for planning and teaching. Second, consulting teachers will find the book useful in their work with teachers in the community.

This book contains the Building Blocks framework—a set of educational practices designed to help teachers do a more effective job of including young children with disabilities and other special needs in early childhood classrooms and programs. The framework provides teachers with a variety of methods and strategies to ensure that children learn important skills in their early learning environments. These practices can be used to complement the curriculum teachers currently use. For example, these practices fit nicely with widely used curricula such as *The Creative Curriculum* (Dodge, 2010; Dodge, Rudick, & Berke, 2006), *The HighScope Preschool Curriculum* (Epstein, Hohmann, & HighScope Educational Research Foundation, 2012), and the second edition of the *Assessment, Evaluation, and Programming System (AEPS®) for Infants and Children* (Bricker, 2019) and support individualization within each curriculum.

The Building Blocks framework is based on research on early childhood inclusion and effective early educational practices (Odom, 2001). For all children, but especially for those children with special learning needs, teachers and teams can and should use educational methods and strategies that are matched to the needs of the individual child. The methods and strategies vary in terms of intensity and specificity. The Building Blocks framework is designed to help teams select the appropriate level of assistance for children. The theoretical and empirical evidence supporting the Building Blocks framework is described in Chapter 2.

IMPORTANT TERMS

The Building Blocks framework uses a vocabulary that may already be familiar to many teachers; however, it is important to clarify what these terms mean in the context of the framework. This section defines several important terms that are used throughout the book.

Inclusion

Inclusion is often defined as the active participation of young children with and without disabilities in the same classroom (e.g., Head Start, child care, preschool) and in community settings. But it is more than that. Inclusion is about ensuring that all children, staff, and families who participate in a program feel supported in that program. In other words, inclusion means that children, teachers, and families feel that they belong to the program and its community. A less traditional way of defining inclusion is to say that inclusion is the celebration of diversity put into action. An inclusive program celebrates what every individual brings to that program and provides each person with the support to be a successful member of that program. Inclusion is defined in a joint statement by the Division for Early Childhood (DEC) and National Association for the Education of Young Children (NAEYC):

> Early childhood inclusion embodies the values, policies, and practices that support the right of every infant and young child and his or her family, regardless of ability, to participate in a broad range of activities and contexts as full members of families, communities, and society. The desired results of inclusive experiences for children with and without disabilities and their families include a sense of belonging and membership, positive social relationships and friendships, and development and learning to reach their full potential. The defining features of inclusion that can be used to identify high quality early childhood programs and services are access, participation, and supports. (2009, p. 1)

Children With Disabilities and Other Special Needs

The term *children with disabilities and other special needs* refers to children who are eligible for special education services and who have individualized family service plans (IFSPs) or individualized education programs (IEPs). It also refers to children who, for a variety of reasons, are struggling in the classroom and need additional help or attention from their teachers.

Individualized Family Service Plan

An *IFSP* is a document developed by the family and the team for a child age birth to 3 years who is eligible for early intervention (EI) under Part C of the Individuals with Disabilities Education Improvement Act (IDEA) of 2004 (PL 108-446). Each plan includes the following: 1) the child's present level of development; 2) a statement of the family's resources, priorities, and concerns; 3) the planned child and family outcomes; 4) the specific EI services to meet the outcomes; 5) a statement regarding natural environments; 6) the length, duration, frequency, intensity, and delivery method for the services; 7) the name of the service coordinator; and 7) the steps toward transition at age 3 years.

Individualized Education Program

An *IEP* is a document prepared for any student, ages 3 through 21 years, who is eligible for special education services. IEPs are required by IDEA 2004. Each IEP states the following: 1) the child's present level of educational performance, 2) the child's annual goals and short-term objectives, 3) the special education and related services to be provided, 4) the extent to which the child will participate in the general education program, 5) the way in which the child's progress will be measured, and 6) the date of initiation and projected duration of services. The IEP also contains a plan for making the transition from high school to adulthood no later than age 16.

Community-Based Classrooms

The term *community-based classrooms* refers to the types of early childhood classroom programs children typically attend. These include child care centers and homes, public school programs, Head Start programs, state and city prekindergarten (pre-K) programs, and private and cooperative preschools. Community-based classrooms do not include specialty clinics, laboratory classrooms, or other specialized schools.

Head Start

Head Start is a federally funded, comprehensive early childhood program that serves children from families with low income. Early Head Start programs serve infants and toddlers younger than age 3 years and their families, and pregnant women. Head Start programs reserve at least 10% of their enrollment for children with disabilities.

Related Services

Related services include physical, occupational, and speech therapy; psychological services; and others that a child with a disability may require to receive the greatest benefit from his or her education. Such services are provided by or under the supervision of certified or licensed individuals (e.g., speech-language pathologist, school psychologist).

Team

Special education and related services are provided by a team. The team consists of family members and professionals who work together to plan and implement the child's educational program.

Early Childhood Education

In this book, *early childhood education* (ECE) refers to educational programs and activities for young children prior to their formal school entry. The ECE teacher is an individual with training and preparation in child development and other content areas related to the education of young children. This individual may have certification in general ECE.

Early Childhood Special Education

In this book, *early childhood special education* (ECSE) refers to educational programs, activities, and services for children with known or suspected disabilities who are ages 3–6 years. ECSE is guided by the requirements of federal and state policies as well as by research on effective educational practices. The ECSE teacher is an individual with additional specialized training and preparation for working with young children with disabilities and other special needs. This individual may work directly with children or in a consulting role. Special certification or endorsement is often required.

Early Intervention

EI refers to services and supports for children with established conditions, developmental delays, and, in some cases, children at risk who are younger than age 3 years, and their families. EI is guided by federal (Part C of IDEA) and state policies as well as research evidence. EI professionals include teachers as well as therapists. Services and supports occur in a variety of settings, with a preference for natural environments.

Universal Design for Learning

The *universal design for learning* (UDL) approach guides teachers in designing learning environments from the very beginning for the widest diversity of learners. UDL encompasses three principles: 1) multiple means of representation to give learners a variety of ways to gain access to information and content, 2) multiple means of engagement to gain and maintain learners' interest, and 3) multiple means of expression to provide learners with a variety of ways to demonstrate what they know (Meyer, Rose, & Gordon, 2014).

Specially Designed Instruction

Specially designed instruction is essentially what special education is all about. This instruction includes organized, planned, and individualized instructional activities needed by a child to accomplish IFSP outcomes or IEP goals and to help the child gain access to the general education curriculum. Specially designed instruction may include changes or adaptations to the content, methodology, or delivery of instruction to meet the child's unique needs.

Tiered Supports

Education has adopted a promotion, prevention, and intervention approach from the field of public health. Such a tiered approach helps to organize teaching and learning for all children in ways that promote development and learning through a high-quality program and research-based curriculum (Tier 1), deploy effective practices to prevent (pre-)academic and behavioral problems (Tier 2), and provide intensive, individualized intervention practices if needed for children who struggle (Tier 3). Universal screening and progress monitoring and collaborative problem solving are key components as well. *Response to intervention* (RTI) and *positive behavioral intervention and support* (PBIS) are other names for tiered supports. Building Blocks is a tiered system of supports (Sandall & Schwartz, 2013).

THE CHILDREN

The stories of five children and their teachers enrich the descriptions of educational practices in this book. The stories help to illustrate the diverse children and families who participate in ECE and also illustrate some of the many ways in which ECE programs are organized.

Nhan is a 4-year-old boy who receives special education services because of delays in language and social skills. He attends a child care center 5 days per week from 7:30 a.m. to 6 p.m. His parents speak both English and Vietnamese. Both parents work outside their home. Nhan and his brother and sister were cared for at home by their Vietnamese-speaking grandmother until Nhan was 2 years old. He then began attending the child care center. His child care teachers became concerned about some of his behaviors and recommended to his parents that he be evaluated. He was identified as being eligible for special education and related services when he was 3 years old. He continues to attend the child care center, and the school district provides an ECSE teacher and a speech-language pathologist who visit the classroom once per week. There is one other child in Nhan's classroom who has an IEP, and another teacher comes to visit that child. Nhan's child care teachers use *The Creative Curriculum for Preschool, Fifth Edition* (Dodge, 2010).

Tina is a 4-year-old girl with a medical diagnosis of Down syndrome and mild to moderate delays in most areas of development. Tina has been enrolled in special programs since she was 2 months old. When she was an infant, home visitors came to her home to provide services. As a toddler, she attended a program at a child development clinic. When she turned 3 years old, she went to a preschool class at a public school. This year, her mother transferred her to the Head Start classroom at the neighborhood center. This is the same program that her older brothers attended. There is one other child in Tina's classroom who has an IEP. An ECSE teacher and a speech-language pathologist visit the classroom and work with the two children and the teachers once per week. A social worker also works in the program. Tina's teacher, Dolores, has taught in Head Start for several years. All of the classrooms and teachers in this program use *The HighScope Preschool Curriculum* (Epstein et al., 2012).

Samisha is a 5-year-old girl with cerebral palsy who lives with her parents, grandmother, and three older siblings. She is learning to use a walker and, when motivated, can move quite quickly. In the classroom, she tends to move around by scooting on the floor. Samisha is very social, and she loves to be the center of attention. Her language skills are slightly delayed, and she does not demonstrate any cognitive delays. Although she is very interested in other children in her class, she is not very successful in peer interactions. She has a difficult time taking turns and sharing materials. She has good dramatic play skills when she suggests the story but has trouble changing her behavior to conform with a plan suggested by another child. Samisha attends a public school pre-K classroom that is team-taught by ECE and ECSE teachers Gia and David. Samisha receives physical therapy once per week in the classroom. The classroom is composed of 15 children: 9 are typically developing and 6 qualify for special education services. The teachers identify their curriculum as teacher created and use their vast collection of ECE activity books as resources.

Drew is a 3-year-old boy who lives with his parents and two brothers, one older and one younger. At 30 months, Drew was diagnosed with autism. His cognitive skills are near age-appropriate levels, but he has significant delays in social and communication skills. He has an extensive vocabulary and can use multiword sentences to express wants and needs, but he rarely makes comments or engages in social conversation. Drew can play independently for a long period of time with a few preferred toys. His favorites are trains, Disney figurines, and markers. He has little interest in and few skills with other materials. Some people consider his play to be repetitive or stereotypical. Drew is also not very interested in his brothers or the other children in his classroom. He is very attached to his mother, however, and seeks her out for comfort and when he wants something.

One of Drew's major challenges is his tendency to have tantrums. He has a very difficult time following even simple adult directions and will often start to have a tantrum if anyone says "no" to him. Drew attends an integrated preschool classroom in a public school and an extended day program specifically designed for children with autism at the same school. The head teachers in both classrooms are trained in ECSE. There are 15 children in Drew's preschool class; 9 children have disabilities and 6 are typically developing. This classroom configuration has been called reverse mainstreaming (explained in more detail in Chapter 3). The extended day program has eight students with autism and four staff members. Between the two programs, Drew is at school for 25 hours per week.

Mateo is an almost 2-year-old boy whose family has a complicated school and work schedule. He is enrolled in a family child care home with six other children who range in age from a few months to 5 years, with a few older children joining for after-school care. The lead teacher and owner, Dara, has operated her child care home for more than 10 years. Mateo's parents, along with Dara, noticed that he was not meeting his early developmental milestones and alerted his pediatrician before his first birthday. He was then referred to the county's EI program and became eligible for services. Although Mateo's global developmental delay does not have a name, he has low muscle tone and does not yet walk. He is attentive to adults and peers but rarely initiates interactions. He uses a few gestures and vocalizations to communicate. Mateo's mother drops him off early in the morning and his dad picks him up in the late afternoon. The visiting early interventionist, Kate, visits every other week at the family child care home and makes an evening visit at

Mateo's home on alternating weeks. Mateo also sees a physical therapist at the EI center once per month. Mateo's older sister receives after-school care at Dara's home. Dara draws from a variety of curricula, state standards, and her own knowledge and experience to create learning activities for the children.

You will learn more about Nhan, Tina, Samisha, Drew, Mateo, their teachers, and their classmates as you use this book. Their stories and the practices described in the book are offered to provide you with support, guidance, and practical suggestions for including children with disabilities and other special needs in your classroom, which can enhance the development and learning of all young children.

Chapter 2

Evidence-Based Practice and the Building Blocks Framework

Evidence, according to the *Oxford Dictionary of Current English, Fourth Edition* (Soanes, 2009), is information indicating whether something is true or valid. Those involved in education and early learning depend on evidence to help determine which interventions will be most effective in promoting children's optimal development and learning. Although the use of evidence-based practices has been a cornerstone of special education for many years, use of evidence-based, or scientifically based, intervention programs in education is mandated by law. The No Child Left Behind Act (NCLB) of 2001 (PL 107-110) required that educational practices must be scientifically based. The reauthorization of IDEA (PL 108-446) states that services should be based to the extent possible on peer-reviewed research. The Every Student Succeeds Act of 2015 (PL 114-95) continues the commitment to evidence-based practice and encourages more local school responsibility for continuous improvement. The idea behind using evidence-based programs in education is really common sense. That is, educators want to know what works best to help children learn and then use only the most effective strategies and interventions. Sometimes, however, determining which strategies and interventions are evidence based is not so easy. Traditionally, research to identify evidence-based practices has involved large studies in which one group of randomly assigned participants receives the special or experimental intervention and a very similar group of randomly assigned participants receives the usual or comparison intervention. One of the problems with this approach to determining the scientific merit of an intervention is that it relies on looking at results for the average participant. This type of study offers information about how groups of participants on average respond to an intervention rather than information about the effects of the intervention on one specific child who comes from one specific family with one specific cultural and linguistic history and who is enrolled in one specific early learning center.

Although this type of research is helpful in identifying some effective intervention approaches, it is not the only strategy that can be used to determine the effectiveness of interventions for young children. Another strategy is to conduct a number of smaller studies, using single subject, mixed methods, or other research methodologies, to evaluate the components of the intervention. This is the approach we used with the Building Blocks framework. Building Blocks, as a package, has not been compared with other comprehensive approaches to preschool inclusion or to comprehensive early childhood curricula. Rather, we have based each of the four building blocks that make up the framework (high-quality early childhood programs, curriculum modifications [CMs], embedded learning opportunities [ELOs], and child-focused instructional strategies [CFIS]) on existing research as well as on our own studies (Odom, 2001) of individual components of the framework.

Understanding the evidence or research support for the specific instructional strategies used is an important component of being an effective early childhood educator. It is even more important to know how to use this information to match instructional programs to the needs of individual students. To truly be a data- or evidence-based teacher, you need to go beyond the research literature and collect information about the learning of your own students and use these data to make decisions about what to teach, how to teach, and where to teach.

In the remainder of this chapter, we describe the Building Blocks framework. You will become familiar with the four blocks as well as with assessment for progress monitoring and data-based decision making, and collaboration—essentials for using the Building Blocks framework. Along the way, we include evidence that supports our approach for helping early childhood teachers provide effective, appropriate intervention for young children.

THE BUILDING BLOCKS FRAMEWORK

The Building Blocks framework evolved from many research activities and experiences in early childhood classrooms. The framework is guided by the goals of successful inclusion and improved outcomes for young children with disabilities and other special needs in community-based programs. Using this framework, teachers can help all of their students participate, learn, and thrive in their classrooms, homes, and communities.

What does "improved outcomes for young children" mean? An outcome is the result or consequence of the supports and services put in place for young children. A valued or meaningful outcome means that a child has received a benefit that improves his or her functioning in everyday life. Federal programs for young children with disabilities (Part C and Part B Section 619 of IDEA 2004) are expected to document the progress children make toward achieving three outcomes, according to the

Office of Special Education Programs (OSEP) of the U.S. Department of Education (Early Childhood Technical Assistance [ECTA] Center, n.d.):

- Positive social-emotional skills (including social relationships)
- Acquisition and use of knowledge and skills (including early language, communication, and early literacy)
- Use of appropriate behavior to meet needs

These global outcomes are in addition to the individual goals and objectives that appear on children's IFSPs or IEPs. Also, children enrolled in Head Start are expected to make progress toward indicators included in the Head Start Early Learning Outcomes Framework (U.S. Department of Health and Human Services [DHHS], 2015). In addition, most states have early learning standards that define the desired outcomes and content of young children's education (http://www.buildinitiative.org/TheIssues/EarlyLearning/StandardsAssessment.aspx).

To accomplish valued or meaningful outcomes for individual children, teachers must match an individual child's goals and objectives with appropriate teaching methods and materials, decide what amount of help or assistance is needed by the child, provide this assistance, and determine whether the assistance was helpful. Fortunately, a number of people (e.g., therapists and other specialists) are available to help the teacher. All of the people involved with a particular child must work together.

In addition, the successful inclusion of young children is based on the assumption that the early childhood settings in which the framework will be implemented are already of high quality—places in which children are nurtured and their developmental and learning needs are met. The first step in using the Building Blocks framework is to assess what is currently happening in the classroom using the Quality Classroom Assessment Form (see Chapter 4, Figure 4.1 and Appendix A); that is, whether the basic features of a high-quality early childhood program are already in place. Assessment is the process of gathering information for the purpose of making a decision. Assessment of the early childhood classroom recognizes the influence of the environment on children's behavior. By assessing the classroom, the education team can determine the extent to which the classroom environment is likely to facilitate children's development and learning. If the assessment reveals that important factors are not present or are not optimal, the team can plan changes in the environment.

Second, the education team considers children's individual goals and objectives. Using an activity matrix is an easy way to consider the individual child's learning objectives when planning classwide activities and routines (see Chapter 4 for more details and examples of activity matrices).

Third, the education team plans for those children who have IFSPs/IEPs or who have difficulty participating in the classroom. Each child should have an individualized plan that takes into consideration his or her particular strengths, interests, and needs. Planning for a child who has disabilities, challenging behaviors, or other special learning needs requires thoughtful teamwork and may also require adaptations to the usual curriculum or more planned opportunities for the child to learn and practice new skills and behaviors.

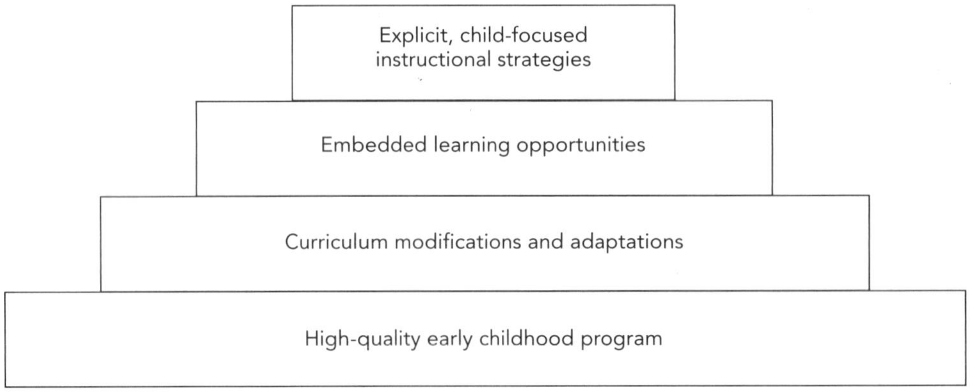

Figure 2.1. The Building Blocks framework.

Figure 2.1 depicts the Building Blocks framework. There are four key components to the Building Blocks framework. The foundation—a high-quality early childhood program—is important for all children. The remaining blocks—curriculum modifications and adaptations; embedded learning opportunities; and explicit, child-focused instructional strategies—represent educational practices that may be appropriate for some children for some of their learning objectives. The framework also indicates that as the blocks become smaller, the intensity and specificity of the practices increase.

The following sections describe each of the Building Block components in more detail. Each section is followed by the evidence base that underlies the component discussed.

HIGH-QUALITY EARLY CHILDHOOD PROGRAMS

A high-quality early childhood program meets principles of developmentally appropriate practice that are based on current knowledge about child development and learning; the strengths, interests, and needs of each child in the group; and the social and cultural contexts in which the children live (DEC/NAEYC, 2009). High-quality early childhood programs and developmentally appropriate practices are described in detail in a variety of resources (e.g., Copple & Bredekamp, 2009; Grisham-Brown & Hemmeter, 2017). Research and experience have uncovered some necessary components of a developmentally appropriate learning environment:

- Engaging interactions
- A responsive and predictable environment
- Many opportunities for learning
- Intentional teaching
- Developmentally appropriate materials, activities, and interactions
- Safe, hygienic practices
- Appropriate levels of child guidance
- Meaningful involvement for families

In other words, a developmentally appropriate environment means a caring community for all learners. These features are necessary, but they may not be sufficient to meet the unique needs of young children with disabilities or other special needs. There are many ways teachers can adjust their curricula to include all children; these are discussed later in this chapter.

Evidence Base for a High-Quality Classroom

A number of large national studies demonstrate that high-quality early learning programs result in better outcomes for children, both immediately and in the long term. Some of these studies were initiated many decades ago and have been following their participants for a long time. For example, the Abecedarian Project (Ramey et al., 2000) was conducted in North Carolina between 1972 and 1977 with children from low-income homes who were enrolled in a high-quality early learning program from infancy through age 5 years. Children who participated in this experimental early learning program tested higher on cognitive assessments on every test opportunity from preschool through age 21. In addition, the students who participated in the experimental preschool had positive lifelong effects: These students were less likely to be enrolled in special education, more likely to attend college, more likely to own their own home, and less likely to spend time in jail.

The Perry Preschool Project (https://highscope.org/perrypreschoolstudy) was conducted in Ypsilanti, Michigan, in the 1960s and had the same overall goal as the Abecedarian Project—to examine the short- and long-term effects of high-quality early learning environments on children living in poverty. The Perry Preschool Project yielded positive effects (Berrueta-Clement et al., 1984; Weikart, Bond, & McNeil, 1978). The children who participated in the intervention preschools scored better on subsequent cognitive testing than children in the same community who did not have access to the high-quality preschools. The results at the age 27 follow-up are also impressive (Schweinhart, Barnes, & Weikart, 1993). Participants in the Perry Preschool study had better jobs, earned more money, were less likely to be receiving assistance from social service agencies, and were less likely to have been arrested.

Another study reinforced the finding that quality in early education matters. The Cost, Quality, and Child Outcomes in Child Care Centers study (Cost, Quality, and Child Outcomes Study Team, 1995) was conducted in the 1990s to examine the relationship between the quality of early learning programs and children's subsequent school performance. Researchers found that children who attended higher quality child care programs performed better in school through kindergarten and that some of these differences were maintained until at least the second grade (Peisner-Feinberg et al., 1999). They also found that children who were at risk for school failure (e.g., students who lived in poverty) were more adversely affected by low-quality preschool programs and received greater benefit from higher quality programs. A number of other studies in the early 2000s have also demonstrated that higher quality early childhood programs can enhance early learning and development for all children (e.g., Barnett, Jung, Wong, Cook, & Lamy, 2007; Yoshikawa et al., 2013).

These findings offer convincing evidence that quality in early learning programs matters. In recent years, new, large-scale public early childhood programs have been launched by States and cities. Federal, state, and local funding contribute to efforts to build high-quality early learning systems and support ongoing evaluation of those efforts. A high-quality early learning program is the foundation of the Building Blocks framework. Extra supports for children with special learning needs are less effective if they are put into place in a setting that does not offer high-quality programming for all children.

CURRICULUM MODIFICATIONS

A *curriculum modification* is a change made to the ongoing classroom activity or materials to achieve or maximize a child's participation. Teachers and other members of the team can make modifications, adaptations, and accommodations to classroom activities, routines, and learning areas to include children with disabilities and other special needs in the classroom and to enhance their participation. By increasing the child's participation and his or her playful interactions with toys and peers, the teacher can help the child take advantage of these opportunities to develop and learn. Of course, if the child is not able to learn through increased participation, the teacher must provide even more help or assistance. Chapter 5 provides more information on and many examples of curriculum modifications.

Think about the five children described in Chapter 1. All of their teachers use curriculum modifications to address some of the children's individual learning objectives. For example, Nhan has a picture schedule to help him remember the daily schedule of events in his classroom. Tina takes a picture or toy with her to recall time so she has something to talk about. Samisha has a large block placed under her feet when sitting at the table to help her sit with better stability. Drew has his name written on his carpet square so he knows where to sit at circle time. Mateo's teacher put a container with his favorite small toys in the sensory table to encourage putting in and taking out.

Evidence Base for Curriculum Modifications and Adaptations

There is a good deal of research on what constitutes a well-designed early childhood environment (for reviews, see Carta, Sainato, & Greenwood, 1988; Hamre & Pianta, 2005; Schwartz, Garfinkle, & Davis, 2002). Use of this evidence base along with the principles of UDL guides teachers and their teams in creating learning environments that welcome every child and family and plan for full and equitable access. Many of the modifications described in our framework help to ensure access for every child. Further, additional individual adjustments may be necessary to meet the needs of individual children.

Wolery et al. (1994) found that early childhood teachers viewed modifications and adjustments to classroom activities and materials as acceptable and feasible. In our own work at the Early Childhood Research Institute on Inclusion, we conducted group interviews with experienced teachers and therapists to identify specific types of modifications (Odom, 2001). These interviews, along with our review of the literature (see Sandall, Schwartz, & Gauvreau, 2016), resulted in the eight categories of modifications described in Chapter 5. Trivette, Dunst, Hamby, and O'Herin (2010) also completed a systematic literature review of various adaptations (e.g., changes to the environment, materials, and/or activities). Adaptations resulted in positive change to targeted behaviors, including improved communication, cognitive, social and motor behaviors, and increased child participation.

EMBEDDED LEARNING OPPORTUNITIES

Teachers can increase or enhance children's learning by embedding or integrating planned opportunities within the usual classroom activities and routines. These planned opportunities are called *embedded learning opportunities* (ELOs). Teachers identify the opportunities most salient to the individualized learning objectives for a child and take advantage of the child's interests by embedding short, systematic instructional interactions into the existing classroom activities and routines to enhance the child's learning. The teacher plans what to say and do and what materials to use within these interactions. ELOs are both teaching and learning opportunities.

All of the children in this book have some of their learning objectives met through ELOs. Nhan gets planned practice at asking simple questions during arrival and snack times. Tina works on sorting by size in the dramatic play area with dishes and at the manipulatives area with the building toys. Samisha works on following the rules in a game by playing games such as Lotto and Candy Land at the games table during free-choice time. Drew gets additional learning opportunities to increase his play skills (using building toys) during free-choice time and small-group time. Mateo gets planned opportunities to use words during diapering, eating, and arrival/departure routines.

The key characteristic of ELOs is that the instructional interaction is planned and embedded, as naturally as possible, within an ongoing classroom or home activity or routine. Planning is also required so that the instructional interaction is repeated; the child must receive sufficient opportunities to learn. The effectiveness of the instructional interaction is evaluated and adjusted if necessary. That is, the teacher monitors the child's progress to find out if the instruction has made a difference. One distinction between ELOs and curriculum modifications is that with ELOs, the individualized objective for the child may be different from, or more specific than, the general goal of the activity or routine. For more information and examples of ELOs, see Chapter 6.

Evidence Base for Embedded Learning Opportunities

A strong evidence base supports the use of ELOs. Snyder and colleagues (2015) conducted a systematic review of the literature of this naturalistic instructional practice, a practice that goes by a variety of names, including ELOs, incidental teaching, activity-based instruction, routines-based teaching, and embedded instruction. Hart and Risley's (1975) work on incidental teaching had an important influence on the development of this practice. Their work, much of which was conducted in Head Start classrooms, showed that children learned more complex language when their teachers systematically embedded teaching interactions into classroom routines. Effectiveness is maximized by embedding and distributing instruction throughout activities and routines (Wolery, 2005).

The Snyder review as well as earlier reviews by Hepting and Goldstein (1996), Horn and Banerjee (2009), and Rule, Losardo, Dinnebeil, Kaiser, and Rowland (1998) found that embedded instruction is an effective way to teach targeted skills across curricular domains. A variety of specific instructional practices are used, with most employing prompt and prompt-fading procedures as well as reinforcement techniques (e.g., Daugherty, Grisham-Brown, & Hemmeter, 2001; McBride & Schwartz, 2003). Some studies also found improved generalization (e.g., Wolery, Anthony, Caldwell, Snyder, & Morgante, 2002). This means that children are able to demonstrate the target skill across a variety of settings. Teachers view embedded instruction favorably (e.g., Horn, Lieber, Li, Sandall, & Schwartz, 2000). Professional development is also useful in helping beginning and experienced teachers use embedded instruction (e.g., Phillips & Halle, 2004; Snyder et al., 2018). The important lesson running through all the evidence about the practice of ELO is that children's learning is related to teachers' planning of ELOs, use of multiple opportunities to learn and practice, and providing quality instructional feedback.

EXPLICIT, CHILD-FOCUSED INSTRUCTIONAL STRATEGIES

Sometimes, more explicit instruction is needed than is given through curriculum modifications or ELOs. Using child-focused instructional strategies (CFIS), ECE teachers or other specialists identify learning opportunities matched to a child's individual objectives and provide planned, consistent, systematic instruction to teach specific skills, behaviors, or concepts. These skills, behaviors, or concepts may be ones that the child is not able to learn from the usual curriculum, even with modifications or ELOs; or these may be skills, behaviors, or concepts that are unique to the child.

All of the children's teachers use CFIS to address some of the children's learning objectives. Nhan receives instruction to increase his English vocabulary every morning. He asks a classmate to join him so that he can use his new words in conversation. Tina receives special instruction during her toileting time, in which she works on unfastening and fastening her clothing. Samisha has a specially planned instructional program to teach her to sustain interactions with peers. This program occurs every day at the beginning of free-choice time in the dramatic play area. Drew works on taking turns in conversation with peers at his small-group table. His teacher uses a systematic prompting strategy to increase the number and complexity of turns. Mateo's teacher strategically places cube chairs on her covered patio. She uses verbal and physical prompts to elicit Mateo's "cruising" from chair to chair and reinforces his attempts to give him more systematic practice in upright mobility.

With CFIS, instructional interactions are even more systematic and more intensive than when using curriculum modifications or embedding more learning opportunities. Whereas the use of curriculum modifications and ELOs allows the teacher to continue to make use of ongoing activities and routines, CFIS are used when the child's individual objectives and learning needs are such that the objective drives the teacher's planning. The focus of instruction is on foundational skills that the child has not mastered, prerequisite skills, or barrier behaviors that interfere with learning. Many of the same instructional strategies that are used to deliver ELOs are used for CFIS; however, the specificity and intensity of instruction are greater, and the child's learning activity may look different from the learning activity for other children in the classroom. Chapter 7 provides more information about CFIS and when to use them in the early childhood classroom.

Evidence Base for Child-Focused Instructional Strategies

Of all the blocks in the framework, CFIS have the most robust research support (see Collins, 2012; Wolery, 2005; Wong et al., 2015). The majority of this support comes from single-subject research that demonstrates the effectiveness of such teaching strategies as positive reinforcement, response prompting, peer mediated instruction, and corrective feedback. Much of this research involves people with disabilities; however, one striking exception to this is one of the first research studies, published over 50 years ago, documenting the effectiveness of the use of positive reinforcement to increase appropriate social behavior. Eileen Allen and her colleagues (1964) systematically used positive teacher attention to increase the social interaction of a preschooler who was typically developing but who avoided his peers. The intervention was simple but effective. The teachers stopped interacting with the child when he was playing alone. When he was playing with or near other children, they would interact with him, encourage him, and provide lots of positive reinforcement. In a matter of weeks, the child was playing with his peers, and the teachers were able to decrease the amount of encouragement they provided. Playing with his friends became reinforcing to the child and was all of the encouragement he needed.

CFIS are used successfully to teach greater independence, skills for acquiring and using knowledge, positive peer relationships, and appropriate behavior in a variety of settings. Diane Sainato and her colleagues (1990) used CFIS to teach students to increase their ability to work independently on a number of preacademic skills. Using explicit instruction and positive reinforcement, they taught young children to monitor their own on-task behavior. This self-monitoring strategy, an important skill for success in school and work, helped students increase the amount of time they were able to work independently and enabled them to complete more age-appropriate tasks.

Using peers in the classroom to help children learn is another area with strong research support. Phil Strain and his colleagues (Strain & Bovey, 2011; Strain, Kerr, & Ragland, 1979) have documented the effectiveness of peer-mediated interventions, primarily among children with autism and children who are typically developing. They have demonstrated that children with autism learn and maintain important social interaction skills and that children with and without disabilities have positive long-term effects from the intervention (Strain & Hoyson, 2000). Susan Fowler and her colleagues (1986) conducted a series of peer-monitoring studies in which children with and without behavior problems took turns acting as the peer monitor and receiving feedback. They found that both giving and receiving feedback were related to improved outcomes for all participants.

Results are even more striking from research that has examined the effects of combining explicit instruction and a peer-mediated intervention, such as peer tutoring. Simmons, Fuchs, Fuchs, Mathes, and Hodge (1995), for instance, investigated reading instruction among young elementary school children who were at risk for reading failure due to either poverty or disability. They compared the use of explicit instructional strategies alone (similar to CFIS) with explicit instruction and peer tutoring. Although children in both of these groups made meaningful gains in reading, the group that received the explicit instruction plus the peer tutoring made more progress. This study illustrates the effectiveness of combining instructional approaches to meet the learning needs of young children.

ASSESSMENT AND PROGRESS MONITORING

Ongoing assessment of child performance is a key feature of the Building Blocks framework and a recommended practice (DEC, 2014). Information about a child's performance relative to valued outcomes—both the child's individual outcomes and those deemed important for all young children—is gathered and used to make decisions about what to teach and how to teach. To make good instructional decisions, the teacher and the team collect information about the child's performance within the context of his or her usual learning environments, such as the classroom, the playground, and the home. The teacher and the team regularly monitor the child's progress through systematic data collection to see how the child is responding to the supports provided (e.g., curriculum modifications, embedded teaching, more intensive instruction). They then use this information to make decisions about the child's continued need for instructional support. Chapter 4 introduces methods for collecting and using child progress information.

COLLABORATION

The effective use of the Building Blocks framework requires that teachers and other team members work together through the process of collaboration. Collaboration is the cornerstone of effective inclusion (Lieber et al., 1997; Odom, 2001) and a recommended practice (DEC, 2014). Collaborative teams hold shared beliefs, work toward common goals, have varying areas of expertise, use collaborative skills, and share the work involved in helping children move toward their goals. It is necessary to collaborate with family members as well as with other early childhood specialists to optimize child outcomes.

The five children, Nhan, Tina, Samisha, Drew, and Mateo, are enrolled in a variety of classrooms with a variety of teaching arrangements, yet all of their teachers work collaboratively with other team members. These teams differ in membership depending on the goal of or reason for the collaboration. Nhan's teachers, a consulting teacher, a speech-language pathologist, and his parents meet regularly to plan for and discuss his progress in learning to communicate with adults and peers. Tina's teacher, Dolores, and the assistant teacher, Maggie, meet together at the end of every school day to talk about the day and to plan Tina's next school day. Samisha's teachers and the physical therapist meet every other week to talk about her progress. Drew's teacher, Jennie; Jennie's assistant, Marlene; a speech-language pathologist; an occupational therapist; Drew's mother; and a behavior specialist meet to develop a plan to decrease Drew's tantrums. Mateo's early interventionist visits his home and his family child care home and organizes virtual meetings that also include his physical therapist. For each of these children, their teachers, parents, related services providers, and school or program administrator meet together to develop the child's IFSP/IEP.

Collaborative skills can be difficult to acquire and require a good deal of practice, but these skills are essential for successful inclusion. Chapter 3 provides more information and strategies to enhance collaboration among the people who care about young children.

SUMMARY

This chapter introduces the structure of the Building Blocks framework and describes the evidence base that supports it. The aim of the framework is to help teachers identify, plan, and use educational practices that provide individual children with the assistance they need to develop and learn within their early childhood classrooms. Like a response to intervention (RTI) approach, Building Blocks provides teachers with strategies for determining whether children are making progress and information on how to provide additional support if they are not. Building Blocks is compatible with RTI and other tiered approaches to intervention (Buysse & Peisner-Feinberg, 2013). Building Blocks gives teachers a practical, feasible, and evidence-based approach to meeting the needs of all of their children and providing specialized instructional support for individual children who need it.

The Building Blocks framework is consistent with the DEC's Recommended Practices that provide guidance on effective practice based on empirical evidence as well as on the wisdom and experience of the field (DEC, 2014). Although it is important to ensure that the instructional strategies being used in the classroom are grounded in strong research evidence and that teachers are familiar with that evidence, it is also important not to assume that just because an intervention is supported by research evidence it will automatically be effective with every student. Teachers need to collect and analyze data on instruction that occurs in the classroom and use those data to make decisions about a child's educational program.

The Building Blocks framework requires that teachers and teams work together to 1) provide a high-quality education for all children, 2) watch for children who are not making progress, 3) provide the amount and type of support(s) each child needs using teaching strategies that are likely to be effective, and 4) carefully monitor all children's progress. Subsequent chapters offer more information about each of the educational practices described in this chapter and the tools needed to put them into action.

Chapter 3

Keys to Collaboration

Collaboration means working together to make something, to solve a problem, or to reach a shared goal. Reviews of the literature on early childhood inclusion have identified a number of synthesis points, and one clear point is the repeated finding that collaboration is the cornerstone of effective inclusive programs (Barton & Smith, 2015; National Professional Development Center on Inclusion [NPDCI], 2009; Odom, 2001). This means that the adults, including professionals, parents, and other adult caregivers within and across systems and programs, need to talk and work with each other. At the same time, collaboration among adults from different professional disciplines and often representing various programs, agencies, and perspectives is one of the greatest challenges to successful implementation of inclusive practices.

Early childhood programs and services are situated within a larger and sometimes complex ecological systems context. Young children attend all sorts of early education and care programs such as Head Start, public and private preschool, and child care in homes and centers. Children with disabilities are enrolled in all of these programs. Administrative coordination and support are important for inclusion to be successful. Our focus in this chapter is on collaboration among those who work directly with children and families. However, teachers and team members need to recognize and appreciate the potential differences across programs, agencies, and people, in terms of procedures, funding, and philosophy, as they grapple with the day-to-day effort of working together to meet the needs of each child.

Members of any collaborative team will bring various cultural, linguistic, and experiential perspectives to the work of interaction with and problem solving as a team. Team members may have differing ideas about disability, school, inclusion, the role of professional helpers, behavioral expectations for young children, and many other concepts and practices. In addition, team members will have differing amounts of time available to develop partnerships, including partnerships with family members. All of these features influence team functioning. Team members will need to respect the values and beliefs of all members and demonstrate awareness of and appreciation for differing points of view. Team members should be open to considering adaptations and alternative ways to solve problems and deliver services. Interpreters and trusted guides can be valuable members of some teams. There are other ways to individualize team functioning. Professional team members are encouraged to practice self-awareness and reflection and be open to opportunities to learn about cultural and linguistic sensitivity.

Collaboration takes time, and it takes a willingness to develop the respect and trust necessary for establishing productive relationships among team members. Effective collaboration supports higher quality instruction overall and enables teams to individualize and meet children's diverse learning needs. Among the features of collaboration for successful inclusion are the following:

- Adequate time for the team to meet
- Time to develop trusting relationships
- Clarity of roles and respect for others' contributions
- Effective and frequent communication, and appreciation for variations in the customs and preferences in communication and interaction
- Shared responsibility for all children
- Participation of all team members
- Ability to identify goals and develop strategies to meet them

HOW TO FORM A COLLABORATIVE TEAM

When forming a team, it is helpful to first determine the team model you will be using, the goals of the team, and the team's membership. Inclusion exists in many forms, and special education services use many different models based on the location of the program (e.g., public or private, home or center) (Odom et al., 1999). In addition, the ways in which specialized services are designed and delivered may vary. Table 3.1 lists and describes some of these models. The Building Blocks framework may be applied within all of these models.

Continue by clarifying the function(s) of the team. Teams often expand or contract to meet particular purposes and to address particular goals. Having shared goals is fundamental to a well-functioning team. Identification of team goals will also guide the team's membership. Team members may include the teacher(s) as well as classroom assistants or paraprofessionals; related services personnel such as physical therapists, occupational therapists, speech-language pathologists, social workers, and other specialists; the child's parents or guardians; and the program administrator. For purposes such as IFSP or IEP planning, the team may be large, and membership is determined, in part, by legal requirements. For other goals, such as ongoing curriculum and lesson planning, the team may be smaller.

Table 3.1. Inclusion models

Service model	Description
Team teaching	An ECE teacher and an ECSE teacher jointly plan for and implement instruction in a classroom that includes children with and without disabilities.
Consultation	The ECE teacher provides most of the instruction in the inclusive classroom. An ECSE teacher comes to the classroom to consult on a regular basis.
Reverse mainstreaming	An ECSE teacher is the lead teacher in a classroom that includes children with and without disabilities.
Integrated activities	The ECE teacher and the ECSE teacher have separate classes. They bring the children together for joint activities on a regular basis.

Key: ECE, early childhood education; ECSE, early childhood special education.

STRATEGIES FOR MEETING AS A TEAM

Teachers say that finding time to meet is one of the most difficult problems they face. Here are some ideas that teachers have shared for meeting times:

- Some teachers like to meet before the children arrive or after the children leave.
- Others meet during naptime.
- In one program, all of the children had motor time with the adapted physical education teacher once per week. During that time, the other staff members held a team meeting.
- In one district, schools had an early release day once each week. That time was used for team meetings.
- At another large early childhood center, a floating substitute teacher took over a classroom so that the general classroom teacher could attend meetings and conferences.

Telephone, e-mail, video conferencing, and various tele-communication applications can be useful communication tools to assist in the collaboration process, especially for inter-agency and community collaboration. Advances in technology have enabled teams to store meeting notes electronically and share these with all team members. However, it is important that the team has some face-to-face meeting times because these enhance the development of trust and understanding of others' perspectives. In particular, it is important that newly constituted teams come together to orient each other to the process of clarifying professional roles and the purposes and goals of the team.

HOW TO STRUCTURE A MEETING

Team meetings can range in the degree of formality or structure. Daily debriefings with the teacher and classroom assistants may be relatively informal, whereas IFSP or IEP meetings may be much more formal. However, once a team is organized and has established meeting times, the general structure or framework of the meetings should be devised to ensure that they run smoothly and productively. Although the following steps may seem somewhat rigid for team members who work together every day, the added structure is valuable for helping members who are present less often or are members of many different teams to truly and actively participate.

The first step is to choose roles for the team meeting. These roles may rotate from one meeting to the next. At each team meeting, choose a facilitator. The facilitator helps create the agenda and assigns times to agenda items, keeps the meeting moving and on topic, and solicits participation from each team member. Each meeting also needs a recorder to note what happens during the meeting, including all decisions that are made, and to record who is responsible for specific follow-up activities. The recorder makes sure that everyone gets a copy of these notes prior to the next meeting. Finally, every meeting needs a timekeeper to make sure that the meeting starts and ends on time and to let team members know when time is up for discussing each item on the agenda.

The second step is to set the agenda. The facilitator takes the initiative in setting the agenda. He or she begins by summarizing the results of the last meeting as set forth by the last meeting's recorder. Then, the facilitator identifies the purpose for this meeting and works with the team to decide what should be discussed to achieve the purpose. The minutes of the last meeting can serve as a prompt for remembering any unfinished business. If an agenda item refers to changing or altering a child's learning objectives or instructional approach, it is essential that the child's performance data be shared at the meeting. Team members take responsibility for bringing needed information to each meeting.

The third step is the discussion of the agenda items. This should take up the greatest portion of the meeting time, and ideally everyone in the meeting participates during this step. The facilitator should solicit participation from anyone who is not speaking up. Sometimes, this may mean encouraging team members to confront areas of disagreement. The facilitator is also responsible for keeping team members moving toward the stated purpose of the meeting and redirecting team members who digress from the topic. Toward the end of the discussion of agenda items, the facilitator should restate, reflect, and summarize the discussion, and whenever a decision is imminent, he or she should summarize the decision for the team. This allows team members to hear the decision articulated in someone else's words and can help clarify any miscommunication.

The final step is ending the meeting. During this step, the facilitator, with the help of the recorder, makes sure that all team members know what tasks need to be accomplished before the next meeting. More information about how to structure a meeting can be found in Friend and Cook (2013).

ACHIEVING YOUR TEAM'S GOALS

Before teams begin to work toward their goal, they should be sure that all team members share an understanding of what the goal means and how they will know when the goal has been met. For example, an ECE teacher and an ECSE teacher are working together using the team teaching model; their goal for the meeting is to plan learning activities for the classroom. They first need to agree about what "plan learning activities for the classroom" means to them. An exercise that can help team members reach a mutual understanding of the goal is to have them consider specific questions. For this example, listed here are some of the questions the team members might ask themselves:

- Will we write lesson plans together?
- Will we be responsible for jointly delivering the instruction?

- Will the ECE teacher plan each activity and the ECSE teacher plan the modifications?
- Will the ECE teacher and the ECSE teacher take turns and plan independently for certain activities or days?

There are no right answers to these questions. The point of this exercise is for the team members to agree about the meaning of the goal. This team may decide to meet each Friday afternoon and produce joint lesson plans for the following week. They will know they have met their goal when they leave the meeting with completed plans that all will use.

THE PROBLEM-SOLVING PROCESS

Team members often must identify and solve problems that arise in trying to meet their goal. The following problem-solving steps are described in detail by Friend and Cook (2013):

1. Identify the problem.
2. Generate solutions.
3. Evaluate the solutions.
4. Implement the solution you choose.
5. Evaluate the outcome.

Tina's team is made up of her ECE teacher, Dolores; the assistant teacher, Maggie; the consulting ECSE teacher; the consulting speech-language pathologist; the program's social worker; and Tina's mother. They are using the consultation model, and the goal is to include Tina in all classroom activities. They are meeting because Tina often refuses to walk from the playground to the classroom, which constitutes a barrier to the team's expressed goal.

Step 1. The first step, problem identification, is probably the most important step in the process. The team needs to define terms, as was done in the goal statement, so that all team members are in agreement.

When this team came together, they needed to refer to Tina's classroom data and respond to questions such as the following:

- How does Tina refuse?
- What does she do and say?
- How long does the situation last?
- How often does the behavior occur?
- Does it happen at any other time?
- Does Tina make other transitions independently?
- What is the same and what is different about this transition?
- What do the adults do?

Step 2. Once the team members reach a consensus regarding the problem, the next step is generating solutions. Friend and Cook (2013) described three different approaches that can be used to generate solutions: brainstorming, brainwriting, and nominal group technique. These approaches allow the team to generate many potential solutions to the problem before settling on one solution.

During *brainstorming*, team members verbally call out potential solutions. No solution is evaluated during the brainstorming stage, and the team members state as many solutions as they can think of. *Brainwriting* is similar, but each team member first writes down potential solutions and then shares them with the group. Using the *nominal group technique*, each team member writes several potential solutions. Then, team members share one solution at a time and take turns sharing until all solutions have been presented. The recorder lists each solution, and team members rate each solution on a scale from 1 to 5 (*least preferred* to *most preferred*).

Step 3. Now, the team is ready to evaluate the potential solutions that have been generated. One way to do this is to list or describe the positive and negative features of each solution. Team members should remember that some solutions may require additional authority (e.g., allocating funds, changing job responsibilities). The team should select one of the possible solutions to use during their problem-solving session.

Here are the potential solutions generated by Tina's team:

- Pick her up and hold hands while walking back to class.
- Let Tina ride in a wagon.
- Use a peer buddy to walk with Tina.
- Let Tina carry a favorite toy back to class.
- Make sure that Tina's favorite activity is available when she gets to class.
- Let Tina walk with her favorite teacher.
- Wait with her without talking until she stands up and walks to class.
- Give Tina some kind of tangible reinforcer when she gets to class.

Following their discussion of the positives and negatives of each potential solution, the team decided to try using a peer-buddy system. Next, they assigned tasks to be accomplished:

- Dolores will talk with a few classmates to recruit them to be Tina's partner.
- Dolores or Maggie will remind Tina at the end of playground time that it is time for her to pick a buddy.
- The consulting ECSE teacher will make a picture card that has photos of Tina's buddies from which she may choose.
- The consulting ECSE teacher will make a simple data collection chart.

Step 4. It is time to implement the selected solution and collect data. Designate a trial period as a way to try out the solution.

Step 5. At the end of the specified trial period, the team summarizes the data to see whether the solution worked. If it did, the team will continue with it.

If not, the team will meet again, following the same steps, and decide on another option. The team can use the Evaluation Worksheet (see the blank form in Appendix A) to keep track of the plan and to evaluate it.

This example illustrates the use of collaboration skills and team-meeting skills when the "problem" is a challenging behavior. The same approach works for other learning challenges. For example,

Nhan's team has been embedding opportunities for Nhan to learn new words during free-choice time. However, the team is concerned that his vocabulary is not increasing. His teacher and speech-language pathologist put their concern on the team agenda and will bring Nhan's performance data to the meeting.

Or,

During a home visit, Mateo's parents comment that he doesn't seem to be making much progress in walking. Mateo's early interventionist organizes a meeting with Mateo's parents; Dara, his child care provider; his physical therapist; and herself. In person and via video conference, the team members examine Mateo's progress on walking and then make adjustments to their current plan.

SUMMARY

Successful adult collaboration contributes to successful inclusion of young children and enables the individualization that meets each child's needs. In this chapter, we presented ways and strategies that help adults effectively work together. Collaboration takes real effort and means working across agencies and boundaries.

The early learning landscape has changed over the past several years. In particular, public early childhood programs have expanded. With that expansion has come increased scrutiny as to what constitutes high-quality early care and education. A high-quality program should be one that is inclusive of children with disabilities and other special needs and their families. This requires collaboration at the state and community level as well as within the child's own program or classroom.

Chapter 4

Getting Started

The Building Blocks framework is designed to help teachers identify concerns in the early learning setting and plan strategies for helping a child develop and learn when the child is having trouble meeting his or her individual learning objectives. The format is appropriate for any child who experiences repeated challenges, such as not attaining learning objectives or displaying excessive behaviors that interfere with the child's own learning or the learning of others. The Building Blocks framework can also be used for children who are identified for special education services and who have IFSPs or IEPs.

This chapter describes the procedures for using the Building Blocks framework in early childhood classrooms. These step-by-step procedures guide the team from the initial concern (e.g., how to teach the individual learning objectives, what to do about a challenging behavior) to a useful plan. The goal is to help the team transform the IEP, other individual plan, or concern into actual teaching and learning opportunities in the classroom. This chapter helps the team with the following:

- Assess the classroom to ensure that it provides a high-quality learning environment for all children
- Identify and clarify the classroom schedule
- Gather information on children's individual goals and objectives
- Assess the learning needs of a child who concerns the team
- Clarify the concerns about the individual child
- Create a plan

Table 4.1. The Building Blocks Blueprint

Implementation steps	Forms and information resources
Step 1. Assess the quality of the classroom	Quality Classroom Assessment Form (or another assessment of the environment) Classroom Action Worksheet
Step 2. Plan the classroom schedule	
Step 3. Plan for an individual child	Child's Individualized Education Program (IEP), Individualized Family Service Plan (IFSP), or Behavior Support Plan Results from classroom-wide curriculum assessment Child Assessment Worksheet
Step 4. Clarify the problem, issue, or concern	Planning Worksheet
Step 5. Create plans	ELO-at-a-Glance (see Chapter 6) Instruction-at-a-Glance (see Chapter 7)
Step 6. Construct an activity matrix	Child Activity Matrix Classroom Activity Matrix
Step 7. Implement and evaluate the plan	Evaluation Worksheet

- Construct a Child Activity Matrix that shows when the plan will be used
- Implement the plan
- Evaluate the plan and monitor child progress

Many forms are included to help teams reach these goals. Although forms are provided, teams should use only those that work for them—it is not necessary to use each of these forms. This chapter contains filled-in forms; blank forms that teams can photocopy and use are in Appendix A. The following sections describe each of the steps. Table 4.1 serves as a guide to the forms that are appropriate for each of the Building Blocks steps.

STEP 1: ASSESSING THE QUALITY OF YOUR CLASSROOM

The Building Blocks framework and the specialized practices described in this book, such as curriculum modifications and child-focused instructional strategies (CFIS), are built on the foundation of a high-quality early childhood program. Classroom quality is linked to child outcomes. Therefore, the first step in using the framework is for the teacher or classroom team (i.e., the people who know the classroom well) to assess the early childhood classroom for 10 basic quality indicators using the Quality Classroom Assessment Form. It is especially helpful to list examples for each of the 10 indicators on the form. The results of the assessment will indicate whether the classroom is interesting and engaging to children, offers a balance of activities and learning arrangements, and provides children with both physical and emotional security. Figure 4.1 shows how Tina's (described in Chapter 1) teachers completed the form for their classroom.

Some teachers or teams may already use another rating form to assess the classroom environment or as part of an accreditation process—for example, the Environment Rating Scales (Harms, Clifford, & Cryer, 2015; Harms, Cryer, & Clifford, 2007; Harms, Cryer, Clifford, & Yazejiam, 2017) or the Classroom Assessment Scoring System (CLASS; Hamre, LaParo, Pianta, & LoCasale-Crouch, 2014;

Quality Classroom Assessment Form

Date: 1/16

Classroom: Head Start

Team members: Dolores Sherman (teacher) Maggie Ong (assistant teacher)

Goal: Assess the classroom environment

Indicator	Yes	No	Not sure	Examples
1. Do children spend most of their time playing and working with materials or with other children?	X			Children are busy and active most of the time.
2. Do children have access to various activities throughout the day?	X			We schedule different sorts of activities.
3. Do teachers work with individual children, small groups, and the whole group at different times during the day?	X			Scheduled small groups and snack; meeting times with whole group; individual time during plan-do-recall
4. Is the classroom decorated with children's original artwork, their own writing, and stories they've dictated?		X		Lots of artwork; no writing
5. Do children learn within meaningful (i.e., relevant to their interests and experiences) contexts?	X			Classroom organized for HighScope, learning centers, projects based on children's ideas

(continued)

Figure 4.1. Quality Classroom Assessment Form, as completed by Tina's teacher. (*Source:* NAEYC, 2001.)

Figure 4.1. *(continued)*

Quality Classroom Assessment Form

(continued)

Indicator	Yes	No	Not sure	Examples
6. Do children work on projects and have periods of time to play and explore?	X			Small-group projects; plan-do-recall at their pace
7. Do children have an opportunity to play and explore outside every day?	X			Always scheduled
8. Do teachers read books to children individually or in small groups throughout the day?		X		We read at large group, but not all are interested; book area is not very popular.
9. Is the curriculum adapted for those who are ahead as well as those who need additional help?			X	We use HighScope. We're not sure we're meeting all of Tina's needs.
10. Do the children and their families feel safe and secure within their early childhood program?	X			Most children are happy when they arrive; lots of parents attend parent activities.

Notes: We need to complete the Classroom Action Worksheet for Questions 4, 8, and 9.

LaParo, Hamre, & Pianta, 2012; Pianta, LaParo, & Hamre, 2008). Checklists or guidance materials designed for families to use in selecting a program for their child are also available from sources such as the NAEYC. In addition, the Inclusive Classroom Profile (Soukakou, 2016) is an observation tool that measures indicators of daily classroom practices that support the unique learning needs and characteristics of young children with disabilities and other special needs. Any of these tools will yield information helpful for assessing the classroom environment.

What to Do

Strive to make your classroom a vibrant learning place for all children. If any foundational features are weak or missing, describe actions that the team can take to address the problem. Pay particular attention to the social-emotional climate of the classroom and the instructional supports provided by the teacher(s). The Classroom Action Worksheet (see the filled-in version by Tina's teachers in Figure 4.2) may be used if you answered *No* or *Not sure* to any items on the Quality Classroom Assessment Form. Team members may also use their own experience along with classroom resource books to enhance the classroom. (See the additional resources in Appendix B.) Next, the team implements these actions. This will help to ensure a high-quality environment for all of the children in the classroom.

STEP 2: PLANNING THE CLASSROOM SCHEDULE

One way to help ensure a safe and secure learning environment for children is to have a schedule. A schedule provides a predictable routine for children and should

- Be divided into time segments that are appropriate to the children's needs and abilities
- Offer a balance of active and quiet times
- Provide times for large- and small-group activities and time to play alone or with others
- Include outdoor time
- Offer a balance of child-initiated activities and teacher-directed activities
- Include adequate time for routines (e.g., toileting, snacks) and transitions
- Maximize teaching and learning time and minimize waiting time

What to Do

If the classroom does not have a consistent schedule or if the current schedule is not working, your team should work together to design a new classroom schedule. (For ideas, see Grisham-Brown & Hemmeter, 2017. Other resources are available in Appendix B.)

Steps 1 and 2 are aimed at designing and enhancing the classroom learning environment for all the children. By taking a UDL perspective, the teacher and team provide all children with a variety of ways to access the classroom, curriculum, and

Classroom Action Worksheet

Date: 1/17

Team members: Dolores and Maggie

Indicator*	What's the problem?	What can we do?	Who will do it?	By when?
4. Class decor	We have artwork but no writing.	Ask children to talk about their art. Write their stories, and post with their art.	Dolores Maggie	Start on Monday and continue
8. Book reading	We have storytime for whole group. Not everyone listens or participates.	Make the library corner more interesting. Have an adult in this center to read to small groups and one to one. Add props to storytime.	Maggie will fix the library corner. We'll have our volunteer in library on Wednesdays. Dolores will get new props.	Next week
9. Adaptability of curriculum	Tina doesn't seem to be making progress in her fine motor skills.	Ask consulting special education teacher to provide more information and to break down the objectives into smaller parts. Ask her to demonstrate for us.	Dolores will talk with the consulting teacher and schedule a time during visits so that she can show us.	In 2 weeks

* Abbreviated from Quality Classroom Assessment Form.

Figure 4.2. Classroom Action Worksheet, as completed by Tina's teachers.

learning activities. It is also assumed that the team uses a research-based curriculum guide to develop the rich, engaging, and meaningful learning activities for all the children. See the section on the general early childhood curriculum at the end of this chapter for more on the importance of a curriculum that emphasizes key content.

STEP 3: PLANNING FOR AN INDIVIDUAL CHILD

With an inviting classroom environment and a consistent schedule, the next step is to plan for an individual child. The Building Blocks framework helps teams identify and provide individualized assistance to support a child's active participation and learning. Teams must gather each child's current individual learning objectives. A learning or behavioral objective contains the following components:

- The learner's name
- The behavior
- The criterion (i.e., how many, how often, how much of the time, or how long)
- The conditions

Learning objectives come from at least three sources. First, some children's objectives will come directly from their IFSPs, IEPs, or other individual plans. Second, the curriculum checklist (e.g., the *Assessment, Evaluation, and Programming System [AEPS®] for Infants and Children* [2nd ed.; Bricker, 2019], the Child Observation Record [COR] Advantage [HighScope Educational Research Foundation, 2015], or Teaching Strategies GOLD [Heroman, Tabors, & Teaching Strategies, Inc., 2010]) that is used for all children in the class may help identify an individual child's learning needs. Third, the team's observations of the child's current participation in classroom activities (using the Child Assessment Worksheet; see the blank form in Appendix A) may uncover additional learning needs.

Here are some individual learning objectives Tina's and Drew's teams devised:

- When given a mixed group of objects, Tina will sort all of the objects into smaller groups according to some physical attribute (e.g., color, size) six different times using six different sets of materials (e.g., colored dishes, big and little cars).
- During free-play times, Drew will demonstrate five new play skills (e.g., painting, doing puzzles, building with blocks) on three different occasions for at least 10 minutes each time.

Sometimes, a teacher's concerns about a child seem so overwhelming that it is difficult to clarify the actual problem areas, which makes it even more difficult to design an effective plan. For example, a child may have so many objectives on his or her IEP that the team members wonder how they can possibly find the time needed to work with the child on all of them. Another child may display so many behavioral challenges in the classroom (e.g., running away, grabbing toys, yelling) that the adults feel that they are spending all of their time trying to regain order. Or sometimes, the child's IFSP outcomes or IEP goals are drawn from standardized measures and seem unrelated to the classroom or daily life.

The Child Assessment Worksheet can help pinpoint your concerns for a particular child and link those concerns to the daily routine and ongoing activities. This form guides the collection of information to determine how the child is doing within the context of the classroom and whether the child's learning needs are being met.

Drew's teacher and the rest of the classroom team met together and used the Child Assessment Worksheet to help them plan for Drew (see Figure 4.3). They wanted to incorporate his IEP goals within the classroom activities and routines and to better understand his challenging behaviors.

What to Do

The team should work together to complete the Child Assessment Worksheet. First, fill out the first column with the classroom schedule. Then, in the next column, list classroom expectations for the child in question during each scheduled event. For example, at snack time, do you expect the child to find his or her seat, remain seated, ask for food and drink, and clean up? Do you expect the child to do this on his or her own initiative or with directions from the teacher? Include some of the concepts and skills the child is expected to learn and practice during classroom activities. Each classroom will be different. Doing this as a team helps ensure that all of the adults have similar expectations for children and activities during the day.

In the third column, rate the child's current performance during each of the scheduled activities and routines. Is the child's current performance a strength, average (not a concern), or an area of concern? It is best if the team does this rating together because it allows the team members to share their perspectives and come to a consensus. Note that the Child Assessment Worksheet will work in family child care home settings as well as classrooms. Use the daily schedule of activities and routines. Home visitors and families can identify home routines and use a similar planning process.

STEP 4: CLARIFY THE PROBLEM, ISSUE, OR CONCERN

After compiling a picture of the child's performance throughout the day, think about the following questions: What are the areas of concern? When does the child do well? When do the problems or concerns occur? Which concerns have the highest priority? The Planning Worksheet helps to plan a course of action for meshing classroom concerns with a child's IFSP/IEP objectives within the general early childhood curriculum. The Planning Worksheet is designed to guide the team's discussion of the individual child. The team aims for careful description of the concern (e.g., grabbing materials, not paying attention to the concept being taught, not yet able to manipulate learning materials like crayons or books) and the team's current response. This leads to a problem-solving discussion and the team's best ideas for addressing the concern.

What to Do

The Planning Worksheet has two sections. In Section I, the team completes the IEP Today, which allows the team to use the child's IEP to list the goals and the

Child Assessment Worksheet

Date: 1/17

Teacher's name: Jennie   Child's name: Drew

Classroom activities	Classroom expectations	Child's level of performance
Arrival	Be able to wait with other children until everyone gets off bus. Walk to class with the group without holding teacher's hand.	Strength ___ Average ___ Area of concern X
Circle time	Sit on his mat. Watch the teacher. Participate in songs and fingerplays. Practice counting and learning names. Answer general knowledge questions.	Strength ___ Average X Area of concern ___
Small-group time	Participate in planned activity. Attend to concepts and skills taught in planned lessons. Share materials. Sit at the table.	Strength ___ Average ___ Area of concern X
Free-choice time	Try activities in the different areas. Play with minimal teacher support. Apply concepts and skills. Explore all centers.	Strength ___ Average ___ Area of concern X

(continued)

Figure 4.3. A Child Assessment Worksheet for Drew.

Figure 4.3. *(continued)*

Child Assessment Worksheet
(continued)

Date: 1/17

Teacher's name: Jennie   Child's name: Drew

Classroom activities	Classroom expectations	Child's level of performance
Cleanup and transition	Put away toys when asked by teacher. Match toys to symbols on shelves. Stop playing when asked.	Strength ____ Average ____ Area of concern X
Snack time	Sit at a table. Try food. Interact with peers as appropriate.	Strength ____ Average ____ Area of concern X
Outdoor time	Run and play. Explore equipment. Play near or with others. Share toys.	Strength X Average ____ Area of concern ____
Departure	Follow teacher directions. Take care of clothes and belongings. Walk with the groups to bus.	Strength ____ Average ____ Area of concern X

related current learning objectives. This section can be adjusted for children with IFSPs or behavior plans. It is intended to lay out the child's individual goals and objectives so that the team sees them in relation to the learning needs the team observes in daily routines and typical activities. Section II of the worksheet guides the team to concentrate on the child's participation needs within the ongoing classroom or daily routine. In the first column, list the classroom activities that are areas of concern for the child in descending order of priority based on the Child Assessment Worksheet.

After completing the Child Assessment Worksheet for Drew, the team identified three scheduled activities that were areas of concern (see Figure 4.4). After discussing Drew's needs, his IEP, the needs of the other children in the classroom, and the available resources, the team decided to focus attention on small-group time, free-choice time, and transitions. They reasoned that if they and Drew could be successful during these times, Drew would have many more opportunities to learn and participate in the classroom.

In the second column, describe the problem or concern as carefully as you can. Make your description specific to the classroom activity identified in the first column. Write down exactly what the child does. Sometimes, it is important to capture what the child does *not* do, as well. For example, one child stands or sits by her cubby during free-choice time but never chooses an activity. Another child makes choices and plays creatively with toys but never speaks to the other children; he only nods and points. The team should identify these issues as a collaborative team.

In the third column, describe what the team currently does about the concern. What kind of assistance is provided (e.g., physical help, repeated instructions)? Is it consistent? What sorts of environmental supports (e.g., pictures, models) are currently in place? If the concern is a challenging behavior, how do the adults and children respond to the behavior?

In the fourth column, indicate your plan or your ideas for assistance or instruction. Use collaboration skills (e.g., idea sharing, listening, problem solving) to arrive at your plan (see also Chapter 3). Chapters 5, 6, and 7 contain more information about using curriculum modifications (CMs), embedded learning opportunities (ELOs), and child-focused instructional strategies (CFIS).

These worksheets require teams to discuss and summarize the child's special learning needs, including the child's IEP objectives (or objectives from another individual plan) as well as the concerns identified through an assessment of the child's current level of participation in the classroom. The Child Assessment Worksheet serves an additional function. By identifying the classroom activities or routines that are already areas of relative strength for a child, the team can use those times for embedding opportunities to learn new concepts and skills.

Drew's team—his classroom teacher, her assistant, the speech-language pathologist, the occupational therapist, and the behavior specialist—met together after school to discuss the results of their assessment and to figure out a plan. Drew's mother was not able to join them that day. She sent her notes and asked that Drew's

Planning Worksheet: Section I

IEP Today

Date: 1/17

Teacher's name: Jennie Child's name: Drew

The "IEP Today" is based on the child's complete individualized education program (IEP) and tells the team the child's individual goals and the associated objectives that are the current focus of instruction.

Goal/domain	Current objective(s)
Interacts appropriately with materials during small group activities for 10+ minutes independently	Interacts appropriately with materials during small-group activities for 5 minutes with prompt
Follows routine directions from adult in group setting	Follows 1-step direction from adult in group setting with visual cues
Maintains conversation with peer or adult in topic for 2–3 turns	Responds with words to others' initiation of conversational topics with verbal prompt
Plays in small group with peers independently for 5+ minutes	Shares or exchanges objects with peers on peer request with prompt
Demonstrates five new play skills (different types of play)	Demonstrates one new play skill for 3+ minutes independently
Responds appropriately to variety of general knowledge questions	Responds appropriately to questions about name and age

(continued)

Planning Worksheet: Section II

Date: 1/17

Teacher's name: Jennie   Child's name: Drew

This planning guide will help you collect more specific information for areas of concern for specific children. Using the Child Assessment Worksheet, identify three activities on which you would like to focus your attention. Once you identify the problem, collecting information is the next for instructional planning for children in inclusive settings.

Key: CM = curriculum modification; ELO = embedded learning opportunity; CFIS = child-focused instructional strategy.

Activities	Define concern	What are you currently doing?	Ideas for instruction
Small-group time	Drew grabs materials from children who are seated next to him and needs a great deal of adult attention to stay engaged with the activity.	Drew has an assigned seat at small group, and a teacher sits next to him. When materials are put on the table, he often grabs the most preferred ones and won't share. Then a teacher must intervene.	CM _X_ ELO ___ CFIS ___ Describe: Drew will work independently for at least 5 minutes and respect boundaries telling him what materials are his. We will put his materials on a tray and praise him when he is engaged with his materials.
Free-choice time	Drew will play for a long time with preferred materials but refuses to even try the majority of the materials in the classroom.	Drew is asked to make a choice about where he wants to play. He almost always chooses the trains and cars. When teachers suggest that he make a new choice, he often has a tantrum. Teachers usually let him stay where he is.	CM _X_ ELO ___ CFIS ___ Describe: Drew will go to at least three areas during free-choice time. We will make sure that trains is the last area he goes to and that he can spend the longest time there. Use picture schedule.
Transitions	Drew does not respond to the transition signal if he is at a preferred activity. If he is at a nonpreferred activity, he runs or wanders around the classroom.	A teacher goes to Drew, repeats the instruction, and physically helps with the transition. He often has a tantrum.	CM ___ ELO _X_ CFIS ___ Describe: Drew will use a picture schedule. We will go through the picture schedule at the beginning of the day. At each transition time, we will show him the schedule and repeat the instructions.

Figure 4.4. A Planning Worksheet for Drew.

teacher, Jennie, call her at the end of the meeting. Drew's team summarized current elements of his level of participation:

- Transitions are difficult for Drew.
- He grabs materials and doesn't participate appropriately in small-group activities.
- He has a limited number of preferred play activities; this hinders his participation and learning during free-choice time.

Drew's team also listed his current IEP objectives:

- Interact appropriately with materials during small-group activities
- Follow teacher-given instructions
- Respond to others' initiations of conversational topics
- Share or exchange objects during play
- Demonstrate five new play skills (e.g., painting, doing puzzles, building)
- Respond appropriately to general knowledge questions (e.g., How old are you?)

Drew's team also discussed his performance on his most recent curriculum assessment. His classroom team uses the *AEPS*® (Bricker, 2019) at the beginning and end of each school year.

Because Drew's classroom has several children with special needs, the team wanted to use teaching strategies that were fairly simple but also likely to be successful. They realized that the various adults had tried different approaches and that none of them had been very good at follow-through. Team members knew they needed to be more consistent.

Drew's team decided that a curriculum modification was likely to help Drew keep his materials organized and his hands to himself during small-group time. They also decided that another curriculum modification—a picture schedule—could be used to help Drew participate in free-choice time and to make transitions. As an ELO, the pictures also would be used as a prompt to teach Drew to follow directions. As part of this discussion, the team decided how they would know if they and Drew had made progress. Although Drew's team is large, Jennie and the consulting teacher could use the same process of taking notes and regular debriefing sessions for all other children with special needs in the classroom.

STEP 5: CREATE PLANS

An individual intervention or lesson plan helps teachers and teams describe what they are going to say and do, and what materials they will need to provide the planned instruction focused on the child's individual objective. This is in addition to the classwide lesson or activity plans that are already in place.

What to Do

Two intervention plans are provided. The ELO-at-a-Glance is discussed in Chapter 6, and a blank form is in Appendix A. The Instruction-at-a-Glance form is discussed in Chapter 7, and a blank form is in Appendix A. These forms provide space to detail the child's learning objective, the context for instruction, and a description to guide the instructional interactions. Space for data collection is also provided. Descriptions of CMs are usually inserted into the activity matrix (see the following section), but sometimes teams will create an individual plan for a modification as well.

STEP 6: CONSTRUCT AN ACTIVITY MATRIX

An *activity matrix* helps teachers and teams ensure that teaching occurs. It is difficult to individualize for one child in a busy early childhood classroom. A matrix reminds the team of 1) their planned schedule, 2) the number of children and the number of activities, 3) the number of adults who are available to assist, and 4) the activities that require adult monitoring. These reminders help ensure that the teaching of important objectives is planned and implemented. They also help the teacher and the team use their time and resources in the best ways possible. Gauvreau and Sandall (2018) describe how the activity matrix is used to organize learning activities across various settings.

An activity matrix can be constructed in a variety of ways. Some teams photocopy or print out the form or forms provided in Appendix A and write in the information for their class. Other teams use a computer to construct an activity matrix. Still other teams like to draw a large matrix on art paper and use adhesive notes to fill in the cells. Teams should use what works best for them. It is important for classroom staff to actively participate in creating the activity matrix. When people simply read a matrix prepared by someone else, they are less likely to remember and implement the planned practices. Remember to revise the activity matrix as a child makes progress and objectives and teaching plans change.

What to Do

To make a matrix for one child, write the classroom schedule down the left-hand column. Write the child's name at the top and the child's current objectives across the first row. To make a matrix for several children or the whole class, write the classroom schedule down the left-hand column, and then put the names of the children across the first row. (Activity matrices are used throughout the book as basic planning forms. Look at them carefully. You will see variations of the activity matrix for one child, for many children, and for collecting information about children's progress. Matrices can be created for home routines as well as the classroom.) Use the following codes for the matrices:

CM = curriculum modification

ELO = embedded learning opportunity

CFIS = child-focused instructional strategy

Figure 4.5 shows a Child Activity Matrix for Tina. Figure 4.6 shows a Classroom Activity Matrix for Tina's classroom. This matrix includes two children with IEPs, Tina and Tyrone, and a third child with challenging behaviors, Ricky. Figure 4.7 shows a Child Activity Matrix for Drew.

Child Activity Matrix

Date: 1/17

Teacher's name: Dolores　　Child's name: Tina

Write the classroom schedule in the left-hand column. Write the child's current learning objectives across the top row.
Fill in the appropriate cells with brief versions of the selected teaching strategy.

Key: CM = curriculum modification; ELO = embedded learning opportunity; CFIS = child-focused instructional strategy.

	Use short phrases to request and comment.	Use words to recall action or event.	Respond appropriately during transitions.	Share or exchange objects with peers.	Sort objects by variety of attributes.	Fit things together and take them apart.	Unfasten and fasten clothing (e.g, snaps, zipper on coat.)
Arrival			CM—use picture cards				CFIS—backward chain
Planning	CM—picture schedule of choices		CM—use picture cards				
Work			CM—use picture cards	CM—paired activities	ELO—sort dishes, sort building toys	CM—preferred materials	
Recall		CM—use picture card	CM—use picture cards				
Snack	CM—preferred materials		CM—use picture cards				
Outside		CFIS—use time delay	CM—use picture cards				
Small- and large-group time	CM—preferred materials		CM—use picture cards	CM—paired activities	ELO—plan sorting activities for small group		
Departure			CM—use picture cards				ELO—practice fastening

Figure 4.5. A Child Activity Matrix for Tina.

Classroom Activity Matrix

Date: 1/7 Teacher's name: Dolores

Write the children's names across the top row. Write the classroom schedule in the left-hand column, starting with the second row. Fill in the appropriate cells with brief versions of the selected teaching strategy.

Key: CM = curriculum modification; ELO = embedded learning opportunity; CFIS = child-focused instructional strategy.

	Tina	Tyrone	Ricky				
Arrival	CM—Respond with words, picture cards	CFIS—identify name	CM—Follow routine, picture schedule (all day)				
Planning	CM—request and comment						
Work	CM—share; fit together ELO—sorting (use preferred materials)	CM—play near peers, use preferred materials	CM—Make choice, stay at activity; use picture schedule and timer				
Recall	CM—use words; use picture cards	ELO—use descriptive words					
Snack time	CM—requests, use preferred food						
Toileting	CFIS—fasteners, backward chain						
Outside		CM—play near peers, use preferred social materials	CM—Make choice, picture schedule and timer				
Small- and large-group time	CM—requests; share ELO—sorting (use preferred materials)	ELO—use descriptive words					
Departure	ELO—fastening						

Figure 4.6. A Classroom Activity Matrix for Tina, Tyrone, and Ricky.

Child Activity Matrix

Date: 1/17

Teacher's name: Jennie Child's name: Drew

Write the classroom schedule in the left-hand column. Write the child's current learning objectives across the top row. Fill in the appropriate cells with brief versions of the selected teaching strategy.

Key: CM = curriculum modification; ELO = embedded learning opportunity; CFIS = child-focused instructional strategy.

	Interact with materials.	Follow teacher-given instructions.	Respond to others' conversational topics.	Share or exchange objects.	Demonstrate five new play skills.	Respond to general knowledge questions.	
Arrival			ELO—most to least prompt				
Circle time						CM—invisible support (follow preferred peer)	
Small-group time	CM—environmental support			CFIS—model, differential reinforcement	CFIS—model, differential reinforcement		
Free-choice time	CM—preferred activity is final choice; picture schedule						
Snack	CM—environmental support					ELO—most to least prompt	
Outdoor time				ELO—differential reinforcement			
Transitions		ELO—picture as prompt					
Departure							

Figure 4.7. A Child Activity Matrix for Drew.

STEP 7: IMPLEMENT AND EVALUATE THE PLAN

And now comes the fun part. Try out the plan you have developed for a child in the classroom for at least a week. Happily, plans often work—for example, providing a new toy captivates the child's interest and encourages him or her to join the group; using a favorite colored paper entices another child to the writing center; or pairing a child with a buddy solves the problem of returning at recess. But other times, the plans just do not work. Perhaps it is the other children who like the new toy rather than the intended child, the preferred color has no effect, or you now have *two* children who dawdle after recess. If the plan does not work well, try it for one more day. Use verbal reminders to help the child understand what is expected. Talk up the new toy, the new colored paper, or any other change you have implemented. Make it special. Then observe carefully. Some children need to get comfortable with a change before they try it out. Try again. Remember that what the team was doing before did not work, either. Teaching is a constant process of observing, assessing, making teaching plans, trying them out, monitoring the child's progress, and making adjustments. The excitement is in figuring out what works as well as in the child's accomplishment.

What to Do

At the end of the trial period, answer the questions on a copy of the blank Evaluation Worksheet provided in Appendix A: Did the plan work? What will you do next week? This worksheet suggests three ways to collect information to monitor the child's progress: *counts, notes,* and *products*. *Counts* refers to a record or tally of each time the child exhibits the behavior (also called *event sampling*) or to a record or tally of the occurrence or nonoccurrence of the behavior during a specified time period (also called *time sampling*). Counting works well for recording the occurrence of behaviors: movements that have clear beginnings and ends, such as jumping, buttoning, or asking for more.

Notes involves notetaking or making a written record of the child's performance. You can write down your notes as the behavior occurs or shortly afterward. Notes can be useful for recording more continuous behaviors, such as playing with a toy or conversing with a peer. Notes also provide information about qualitative aspects of the event, such as the child's approach to a toy, persistence, and interest. Always date your notes or indicate on which day of the week the behavior occurred.

Products stands for *permanent products,* which are samples of the child's work. Collect these samples by keeping drawings or other artwork, making audio or video recordings of the child, or taking photographs. It is helpful to write a comment and the date and attach these to the product. All of these performance records can be kept and organized in the child's portfolio, a collection of a child's work that demonstrates the child's efforts, progress, and achievements over time.

Collect information in the way that works best for you and your classroom. The point is to regularly collect and use the information. Remember, it can tell you that the child is learning and that your teaching makes the difference. Figure 4.8 shows a completed Evaluation Worksheet for Drew.

Evaluation Worksheet

Date: 1/17

Teacher's name: Jennie Child's name: Drew

Concern	Plan	Evaluation information
Grabs materials from others and needs a great deal of adult attention	Objective is to work for 5 minutes. Give Drew his own tray and materials. Praise when he is participating.	Counts ____ Notes X Products ____ M—took Molly's glue bottle; Th—no grabbing today Did the plan work? (Yes) No What will you do next week? Drew is participating more fully. Continue with the plan
Plays for a long time with preferred materials but refuses to try other materials	Use a picture schedule with four areas, and make the final area trains and cars. Use timer, and strive for 7 minutes in each of the first three areas.	Counts ____ Notes X Products ____ W—at the sensory table for 3 min, books 4 min, art 6 min. Did the plan work? (Yes) No (Drew did great in the art center!) What will you do next week? Continue
Has a tantrum or wanders at transition times	Give instruction for making the transition. Show the picture. Prompt using slight physical assistance.	Counts ____ Notes X Products ____ (record data on Drew's transition chart) Did the plan work? (Yes) No What will you do next week? Continue

Figure 4.8. An Evaluation Worksheet for Drew.

A NOTE ABOUT THE GENERAL EARLY CHILDHOOD CURRICULUM

A high-quality early childhood program uses a high-quality, research-based curriculum. This curriculum serves as a guide for what to teach (the important content) as well as a guide for planning the day-to-day learning experiences, activities, and interactions that children have with their teachers, their peers, and their environment. A high-quality curriculum is "thoughtfully planned, challenging, engaging, developmentally appropriate, culturally and linguistically responsive, comprehensive, and likely to promote positive outcomes" (NAEYC, 2003. The important content of the curriculum should include social and emotional competence; communication and language development; cognition and general knowledge; physical well-being and motor skills; self-help skills; approaches to learning; and subject matter areas such as science, mathematics, literacy, social studies, and the arts.

Teachers and teams must help young children with disabilities and other special needs gain access to and make progress in the general early childhood curriculum. That is, all children must have opportunities to learn the important content reflected in the early childhood curriculum. To help children be fully included, participate, and learn, teachers and teams need to provide individualized instructional supports for children. The Building Blocks framework is a useful tool for planning these supports.

SUMMARY

This chapter introduces you to the Building Blocks framework for including children with disabilities or other special needs in your classroom. Successful inclusion means that all of the children in the classroom participate, learn, and thrive. Before you can make, implement, and evaluate a plan for doing this, you need to become more familiar with the rest of the book. Deciding whether to use curriculum modifications (CMs), embedded learning opportunities (ELOs), or child-focused instructional strategies (CFIS) takes practice. There are no hard-and-fast rules; it depends on the child, the objective, and the classroom. It is a team decision, so use collaboration and problem-solving skills. Here are some helpful tips:

- If the child needs a little bit of help, try a curriculum modification.
- If the child needs a lot of assistance and direction, try a child-focused instructional strategy.
- If the need lies somewhere in between, try an embedded learning opportunity.
- If your evaluation data tell you that your first attempt was not successful, adjust and try again.

SECTION II

Teaching Strategies

When children are not meeting or accomplishing the important learning objectives that have been identified for them, more support is needed. The chapters in Section II describe educational practices that can be applied when a child is not learning or making progress at expected rates. The practices are grouped according to the type and level of instructional support.

Curriculum modifications and adaptations are relatively simple yet purposeful strategies for altering typical activities, routines, materials, and interactions in order to include children with disabilities and other special needs and to enhance their participation in their environments. The expectation is that by increasing children's participation, their learning is also enhanced. Eight categories of curriculum modifications are described: 1) environmental support, 2) materials adaptation, 3) activity simplification, 4) child preferences, 5) special equipment, 6) adult support, 7) peer support, and 8) invisible support. Examples of the modifications are presented according to category as well as by typically occurring early childhood classroom activities such as ideas for a book corner, block play, and so forth.

If the child is still not making progress on specific learning objectives, then practices are described for providing even more teaching and learning opportunities. We call this level of intensity and specificity *embedded learning opportunities* (ELOs). Specially designed instructional strategies are used and embedded within typical activities and routines. Embedding and distributing instruction are desirable ways for helping children learn valued outcomes and for helping them use new behaviors in a variety of settings and activities. For those children or for those learning objectives that require more explicit instruction, practices are described for clarifying teaching times and for using clear instructions, assistance, and consequences. We call this level of intensity and specificity *child-focused instructional strategies* (CFIS).

Taken together, the practices described in this section build on the foundation of a quality early childhood program. Teachers and teams use their careful observation and assessment of children's learning and, when necessary, match children's learning needs with more specialized, evidence-based, and individualized support to help children learn and thrive.

Chapter 5

Curriculum Modifications

A *curriculum modification* is a change to the ongoing classroom activity or materials in order to facilitate or maximize a child's participation in planned activities and routines. The underlying notion is that increased participation as well as playful interactions with toys and peers will enable the child to take advantage of these opportunities and consequently develop and learn.

Curriculum modifications should be thought of as easy-to-implement interventions that require thought and planning but not additional resources. In fact, many teachers regularly make curriculum modifications without identifying them as such. With careful planning, modifications and adaptations can be important tools in helping children make meaningful progress.

Drew was having a hard time settling down in one spot at the beginning of large-group activities. The children in Drew's classroom all sit on carpet squares during large-group activities. Drew's teacher modified this for Drew by putting his name on his square so that he could be directed to sit at a particular spot in the group.

Samisha sometimes seems distracted by the effort of keeping her balance while sitting in a chair. Samisha has a large block placed under her feet, which helps her maintain her balance so that she can more easily participate in the ongoing activity.

WHEN SHOULD CURRICULUM MODIFICATIONS BE USED?

A modification to the curriculum is most effective when your observations tell you that the child is interested in the ongoing activities but is not able to fully participate. One child may watch the other children and may try to participate without success. Another child may not stay with the activity long enough to take full advantage. Still another child may "tell" you he or she is having trouble with the activity by becoming frustrated, while another child may signal that he or she needs help by becoming withdrawn.

TYPES OF CURRICULUM MODIFICATIONS

Table 5.1 lists eight types of curriculum modifications. The following pages provide numerous examples of each type of modification.

Teachers and therapists who work in inclusive early childhood classrooms have suggested the examples of modifications and adaptations. You may be able to think of others that would also work in your classroom. These modifications are organized in two ways. First, they are organized by type. Second, additional modifications are

Table 5.1. Types of curriculum modifications

Modification type	Definition	Strategies
Environmental support	Altering the physical, social, and temporal environment to promote participation, engagement, and learning	Change the physical environment. Change the social environment. Change the temporal environment.
Materials adaptation	Modifying materials so that the child can participate as independently as possible	Have materials or equipment in the optimal position (e.g., height). Stabilize materials. Modify the response. Make the materials larger or brighter.
Activity simplification	Simplifying a complicated task by breaking it into smaller parts or by reducing the number of steps	Break it down. Change or reduce the number of steps. Finish with success.
Child preferences	If the child is not taking advantage of the available opportunities, identify and integrate the child's preferences	Hold a favorite toy. Use a favorite activity. Use a favorite person.
Special equipment	Using special or adaptive devices that allow a child to participate or increase the child's level of participation	Use special equipment to increase access. Use special equipment to increase participation.
Adult support	Having an adult intervene to support the child's participation and learning	Model. Join the child's play. Use praise and encouragement.
Peer support	Utilizing peers to help children learn important objectives	Model. Pair the child with a buddy. Use praise and encouragement.
Invisible support	Purposely arranging naturally occurring events within one activity	Sequence turns. Sequence activities within a curriculum area.

matched to ongoing activities and routines that typically occur in early childhood classrooms (e.g., art center, snack, sensory table).

Some of these curriculum modifications may be considered assistive technology. *Assistive technology* is a broad term that refers to any item that supports a child's ability to participate actively in his or her school, home, or community setting (Sadao & Robinson, 2010). According to IDEA, all children who are eligible to receive special education or early intervention services are also eligible to receive assistive technology if it is included in the IFSP or IEP. There are additional assistive technology provisions under Section 504 of the Rehabilitation Act of 1973 (PL 93-112) and in the Americans with Disabilities Act (ADA) of 1990 (PL 101-336) that may be relevant for young children.

It is important to remember that a curriculum modification is used to help a child participate. If participating is still not enabling the child to learn, try using an ELO or a CFIS (discussed in Chapters 6 and 7). Remember, also, to evaluate the effectiveness of the curriculum modification. Many curriculum modifications will have a fairly immediate impact. For example, when Samisha's teachers put a block under her feet, they noticed that she sat straighter and more securely and smiled as she played with the toys and materials on the table. Because the purpose of using a curriculum modification is to promote learning, the classroom team should also monitor the child's performance to determine if, in fact, the child is becoming more independent in the activity or routine and if the child is learning the valued content as planned by the teacher for that activity. The Evaluation Worksheet (see Chapter 4, Figure 4.8) is one way to monitor children's progress.

COMMON CLASSROOM CHALLENGES

One reason a child might not participate (or participate successfully) in the ongoing activities and routines of the classroom is that one or more challenging behaviors interfere with participation. At other times, the child may behave in ways that are troublesome to the adults in the classroom. This section covers ways to think about the classroom environment and to modify it as needed to guide children to use behaviors that are more appropriate and adaptive in group learning situations.

One of the features of a high-quality early childhood classroom is the use of developmentally appropriate techniques that can help children learn appropriate classroom and social behaviors. These techniques are called *structural supports* because they involve careful planning or structuring of the environment, schedules, activities, and transitions, with the goal of successful and enjoyable participation and learning in the classroom. Here are several ways to structure the environment for success:

1. *Provide a balance between child-directed and adult-directed activities.* Provide opportunities for children to make authentic choices.
2. *Design a variety of areas in the classroom that are easily viewed and have boundaries.* The teacher should be able to view the entire classroom. The children should be able to recognize the boundaries of the learning areas.
3. *Make sure materials are organized and in good working order.* Materials should be attractive to the children and organized in a fashion that tells children where the materials belong.

4. *Offer activities that provide many ways for children to respond.* Think about the children's current skills and interests. Plan activities that allow choices and different ways to respond.

There are also several ways to structure your classroom schedule for success:

5. *Create a clear and consistent schedule.* Display the schedule in a way that is appropriate for the children, and follow it. Use pictures or photographs as well as words.
6. *Use staff schedules.* Display and use a schedule for the adults that shows them where they should be and what they should be doing.

You can also structure activities for greater success:

7. *Support participation.* Use a variety of ways to help children join activities and sustain participation. Provide a variety of interesting materials to entice children to the activity.
8. *Have high expectations.* With planning and a positive attitude, you can help all children participate and learn new skills and concepts. Plan interesting and appropriately challenging activities.
9. *Be consistent.* Children can be most successful and feel trusted and safe when adults provide consistent expectations and responses.
10. *Give good, clear directions.* Sometimes, that means that you must break down lengthy directions into shorter ones.
11. *When children are participating, provide feedback on their performance and efforts.* Feedback should be sincere and specific.

Transitions can be the most troublesome part of the day because they are often less structured and more difficult for a child to understand than other classroom events. Here are several suggestions for structuring transitions for success:

1. *Teach children your expectations for their behavior during transitions.* Be specific in teaching children what to do during transition times.
2. *Use pictures or other salient cues.* Some children have difficulty following verbal directions, so add pictures or other cues to illustrate what children should do during the transition.
3. *Begin the activity when a few children are ready.* If the activity is interesting and enticing, the other children will join, and those who made the transition quickly will not need to wait.
4. *When in doubt, teach the routine.* If children are still having difficulty with making a transition, teach them—specifically and systematically—what to do and what you expect during the transition.

Even when all of the elements of a structural support base are in place, some challenging behaviors may occur. When this happens, consult Table 5.2, locate the behavior that is occurring, and find the type of curriculum modification that has a high probability of supporting a positive behavior. Then, you can turn to the section in this chapter on that type of modification for ways to develop a plan for the child.

Table 5.2. Ways to address common classroom challenges

Challenge	Environmental support	Materials adaptation	Activity simplification	Child preferences	Special equipment	Adult support	Peer support	Invisible support
Child does not actively participate at large-group time			X	X				
Child refuses to join large-group time	X			X		X		
Child has tantrums during large-group time	X		X					
Child talks out of turn during large-group time	X							
Child is not willing to go to or participate in a certain learning center	X		X					
Child has difficulty making a transition from one area or activity to the next	X			X				
Child is noncompliant when given a direction	X					X		
Child runs in the classroom	X							
Child mouths art materials	X	X				X	X	
Child grabs items from others	X							
Child hits others	X	X						
Child does not pay attention	X							X
Child whines						X		
Child talks back	X					X		
Child engages in self-stimulatory behavior				X		X		
Child engages in self-injurious behavior	X					X		
Child bites others	X	X						X
Child grabs things from others at small group	X							
Child is unstable when walking	X		X		X			
Child has difficulty with descending stairs				X	X		X	
Child has difficulty remaining with the group			X	X			X	
Child dawdles	X			X			X	
Child knows an answer or skill but does not demonstrate it				X		X		
Child refuses to participate in large-group activities			X	X				
Child has difficulty separating from his or her parent	X							

(continued)

Table 5.2. *(continued)*

Challenge	Environmental support	Materials adaptation	Activity simplification	Child preferences	Special equipment	Adult support	Peer support	Invisible support
Child will not remain seated on the bus	X			X				X
Child will not keep his or her seat belt fastened on the bus	X			X			X	
Child screams on the bus	X							
Child screams in the classroom	X							
Child bullies others						X		
Child does not maintain proximity to peers	X			X				
Child is rejected by peer(s)						X		X
Child falls out of chairs	X				X			
Child has difficulty sitting at circle time	X				X			
Child bothers others at circle time				X				X
Child has difficulty beginning and ending projects	X		X	X				
Child has difficulty washing hands		X	X					
Child is not yet using verbal communication (speech)		X						
Child runs out of the classroom	X							
Child eats with fingers					X			
Child does not respond to transition cue	X							
Child does not follow classroom routine	X					X		
Child gives up easily			X	X		X	X	
Child uses toys inappropriately							X	
Child demonstrates low rates of engagement			X	X				
Child has significantly lower skills than rest of class			X					X
Child has difficulty with lining up	X							
Child does not clean up	X		X	X				
Child is easily overstimulated	X		X					
Child throws up or gags easily and/or often			X					
Child will not come to small group				X				
Child mouths inappropriate objects	X					X		

Sometimes, a curriculum modification is not sufficient. Then, you will need to try an ELO or a CFIS. Remember that sometimes children display the challenging behavior because they have not learned a more appropriate or conventional behavior. In many cases, it is a teacher's responsibility to teach that desired behavior.

Some teachers worry that using a curriculum modification may single out a child, may distract other children, or in some way may seem unfair to the other children. The point of using a curriculum modification is to provide individualized support as needed so that each child can participate in the activities and routines of the classroom. If necessary, explain that support is something that helps rather than something special. If other children want to hold a preferred item or try out a piece of equipment, let them try it. There's usually no reason that a modification needs to be off limits to the other children. The teacher and team know that the item is provided or the change is made to offer individualized support. However, other children can use the modification as well.

Curriculum Modifications by Type

This part of Chapter 5 provides numerous classroom examples of each type of modification. You will find the definition of the modification, the general strategy (i.e., what to do), and examples of when the modification might work. There is also space for you to write your own ideas.

Change the physical environment.

If a child pulls things off the toy shelves and then plays in front of the shelves, blocking other children's access . . .

. . . put tape on an area in front of the shelf. Remind children that they must play with the toys outside the taped area.

If a child has difficulty keeping his or her hands to him- or herself when working on individual activities or projects . . .

. . . provide individual workspaces by using trays, box lids, or placemats.

If a child has difficulty with putting toys and equipment away . . .

. . . use pictures or symbols on shelves and containers. Make cleaning up a matching game.

Your ideas:

Change the social environment.

If a child has difficulty playing near other classmates . . .

. . . plan cooperative small-group activities with engaging and highly motivating materials so that the child is close to peers while engaging in fun activities such as murals, cooperative block structures, and so forth.

If a child has no play partners . . .

. . . build friendships by seating a peer next to the child every day at a planned activity, such as small-group or circle time.

If a child is unstable while walking . . .

. . . arrange for the child to hold hands with buddies during transitions. With a buddy on one or both sides, the child will be more stable.

Your ideas:

Change the temporal environment.

If a child does not participate in learning centers during the free-choice time . . .

. . . create a picture schedule for the child. The picture schedule can have pictures or symbols representing the various learning centers organized in a certain order (e.g., art first, dramatic play second, blocks third). The child should be taught to refer to his or her schedule each time he or she finishes an activity or directed to play in a learning center for a specified amount of time.

If a child has difficulty making transitions . . .

. . . just before a transition, provide the child with a picture or an object representing the area or activity that the child should go to next. The child could even take the picture or object to the next area.

If a child quickly finishes with the snack and then has difficulty waiting for the next activity . . .

. . . open one or two quiet centers (e.g., library, computer) after snack time so that the child can leave the snack table when he or she is finished.

Your ideas:

Put the materials at the optimal level for the child.

If a child has to reach up to the counter to put away the dishes and utensils after snack time . . .

. . . place plastic washtubs on child-size chairs or benches for cleanup.

If a child has difficulty standing so that using the art easel is a problem . . .

. . . lower the easel and give the child a chair, or buy or make a tabletop easel.

If a child's feet do not reach the pedals of the tricycle or Big Wheel . . .

. . . tape wooden blocks to the pedals.

Your ideas:

Stabilize materials using tape, Velcro, nonskid backing, and so forth.

If a child's arm movements make the art paper slide off the table...

. . . tape the paper to the table.

If a child has trouble using one hand to hold a toy, and toys (e.g., a jack-in-the-box, hammering toys) fall over when the child tries to use them . . .

. . . use clamps or Velcro to attach the toy to a hard surface.

If a child seems to slip and slide on the wooden chairs in the classroom . . .

. . . attach bathtub appliqués or a section of a bathmat to the seat.

Your ideas:

If the skill or response required by a toy is too difficult for a child, modify the response.

If a child has difficulty turning the pages of a book . . .

. . . glue a small piece of Styrofoam to the pages; this will separate each page, making it simpler to turn them.

If a child does not choose the art center because actions such as gluing and pasting are still too difficult . . .

. . . use Contact paper or other sticky paper as the backing for collages. The child only has to put things on the paper. (Work on gluing and pasting at other times.)

If it is difficult for a child to grasp markers and paintbrushes . . .

. . . wrap pieces of foam around the markers and paintbrushes to make them easier to hold.

Your ideas:

____

____

____

____

____

____

____

____

____

Make the materials larger or brighter to attract the child's attention or interest.

If a child shows little interest in art activities such as making a collage or other activities using paper . . .

. . . include pieces of Mylar or other shiny paper in the collage box.

If a child shows little interest in the storybook during large-group time . . .

. . . use a "big book" or use large illustrations painted or drawn by the children.

If a child with visual impairments has difficulty attending to objects or pictures . . .

. . . use pictures and books that are bold and uncluttered. Use high-contrast colors in visual images.

Your ideas:

Activity Simplification

Simplify a complicated task by breaking it into smaller parts or by reducing the number of steps.

Break down the task or activity into smaller, more manageable parts.

A B C

ACTIVITY SIMPLIFICATION

If when playing with manipulative toys (e.g., puzzles, beads), a child is easily distracted by the pieces and often drops, bangs, or scatters the pieces rather than trying to put the pieces in or on something . . .

. . . hand the pieces to the child one by one. Gradually increase the number of pieces the child has at one time.

If a child is overwhelmed by activities such as cooking projects, craft projects, and table games and is rarely successful at them . . .

. . . break down the activity into several parts. Describe the steps in clear terms. Draw pictures of the steps to make it even clearer.

If a child has a long walk from the car or bus to the classroom and then dawdles, complains, and sometimes stops and drops to the floor . . .

. . . put photos, posters, or other interesting displays at strategic points along the way. Encourage the child to go to the next spot; praise him or her. Then, direct the child to the next spot, and so forth.

Your ideas:

Change or reduce the number of required steps.

If the soap dispenser is on the wall and requires that a child reach across the sink and make an upward motion with the hand, and the child can barely reach it or needs to stand on tiptoes . . .

. . . use a plastic bottle with a pump top as a soap dispenser. Place it on the counter or attach it to the sink with a suction cup.

If a child has difficulty with craft projects that have multiple steps . . .

. . . prepare the craft activity with individual children in mind. Some children may do the entire project. Others may receive projects that have been started, and they do some of the steps.

If a child plays repetitively in the house corner and rarely acts out multiple-step scenes . . .

. . . make photographs of three- or four-step play scenes (e.g., put the pot on the stove, stir, and take it to the table). Use the photos to help the child lengthen his or her play.

Your ideas:

Activity Simplification

Simplify a complicated task by breaking it into smaller parts or by reducing the number of steps.

Break down a complicated task into its parts, and have the child finish with success.

If a child gets mixed up when trying to sort the placemat, dishes, wastepaper, and scraps after snack time . . .

. . . help the child do each step of the cleanup process until you get to the last step. Have the child do this step alone. Gradually increase the number of steps that the child does independently.

If a child has difficulty washing and drying hands . . .

. . . help the child do each step until you get to the last step. The child does this step alone. Gradually increase the steps the child does independently.

If a child has difficulty pedaling the tricycle . . .

. . . help the child place his or her feet on the pedals and start the rotation. Let the child finish the rotation (i.e., push down) by him- or herself.

Your ideas:

Let the child hold a favorite quiet toy.

If a child fusses and tries to leave large-group times such as circle time . . .

. . . let the child hold a favorite quiet toy (e.g., teddy bear, baby doll). Give the toy to the child at the beginning of group time.

If a child has difficulty making a transition from one area or activity to the next . . .

. . . allow the child to carry the favorite toy from one activity to the next.

If a child has difficulty remaining on his or her nap mat during rest time . . .

. . . let the child hold a favorite quiet toy or a favorite book.

Your ideas:

Incorporate the child's favorite activity or toy into a specific area or activity.

If a child does not come readily to circle time or another large-group activity . . .

. . . begin large-group time with a favorite activity, such as blowing bubbles or singing the child's favorite song.

If a child has difficulty paying attention to books, pictures, or table-top materials . . .

. . . incorporate the child's favorite item into the activity as appropriate. For example, if the child likes dolls, make a lotto game using pictures of dolls from catalogs.

If a child has difficulty engaging in new activities or learning centers or perseverates on one activity (i.e., does the same action over and over) . . .

. . . incorporate the child's favorite toy into the area or activity. For example, if a child loves trains and never goes to the dramatic play area, create a train station in the area, or create a fast-food restaurant and use toy trains as the prize that comes with the kid's meal.

Your ideas:

Incorporate the child's favorite person into a specific area or activity.

If a child does not participate in certain learning areas of the classroom—for example, the child rarely, if ever, goes to the library/writing center . . .

. . . assign the child's favorite person to this area.

If a child has difficulty returning to the classroom after outdoor play time . . .

. . . have the child's favorite person tell the child when outdoor play time is over and then walk to the classroom. Have the person tell the child that he or she will see the child again in the classroom.

If a child has trouble staying interested in large-group or circle time . . .

. . . have the child's favorite person lead the final circle-time activity. Introduce this activity while the child is still paying attention.

Your ideas:

Special Equipment

Use special or adaptive devices that allow a child to participate or increase a child's level of participation. This includes homemade equipment or devices as well as commercially available therapeutic equipment.

Use special equipment to increase access to activities and play areas.

If the outdoor play area is a long walk from the classroom, and a child who is not yet a skilled walker takes so long to get to the play area that the child does not have time to use the playground . . .

. . . use a wagon that is big enough for two. Make it a treat to ride in the wagon with the child as well as to pull it. (Make sure the child gets ample practice at walking independently at other times during the day.)

If a child who uses a wheelchair or walker is not able to get close enough to the sensory table to participate . . .

. . . there are a number of possibilities. If the sensory table is strong and sturdy, the child can sit on the table. If the legs on the table can be removed, placing the table on the floor may make it more accessible. Consider giving children individual sensory tables made from plastic bins that can be placed on children's laps, a table, or the floor.

Your ideas:

Special Equipment

Use special or adaptive devices that allow a child to participate or increase a child's level of participation. This includes homemade equipment or devices as well as commercially available therapeutic equipment.

Use special equipment to increase participation.

If a child does not have the hand strength to cut with scissors . . .

> **. . . use loop scissors or other adaptive scissors that require less hand strength.**

If a child has poor sitting balance and seems to use all of his or her energy and concentration to sit in the chair, with little energy left to play with the toys or color or draw . . .

> **. . . make sure the child has a chair with sides or armrests. If the child's feet do not touch the floor, make a footrest out of a sturdy cardboard box or a block.**

If a child sits in an adaptive chair or a wheelchair and during floor activities is not at the other children's level . . .

> **. . . use a beanbag chair or a cube chair in its lowest position so that the child is on the floor with the other children.**

Your ideas:

Provide a model of another way to play or a way to expand on the child's play or other behavior.

If a child repeats the same play actions over and over without making any changes—for example, if a child at the sand table dumps and fills and dumps and fills without seeming to pay attention to the effects of his or her actions . . .

. . . show the child another way to dump and fill, but make small alterations from the way that the child currently plays. For example, hold the container up high while you dump it, or dump the contents through a funnel or short tube.

If you provide props in the block area that are thematic, but the child does not incorporate them into his or her play . . .

. . . take photographs of ways to use the props with the blocks. Place them in the block area, and occasionally draw the child's attention to them.

If a child pounds and pokes at the playdough but does not use any of the tools . . .

. . . take one simple tool, such as a cylinder block. Demonstrate pounding and poking with it.

Your ideas:

Adult Support

Have an adult intervene in an activity or a routine to support the child's participation and learning.

Join the child's play. By being there, you can show your interest and provide encouragement by your presence and through your comments.

If a child goes to the dramatic play area and watches the other children but does little more than observe . . .

> **. . . go to the dramatic play area, see what captures the child's attention, and build on that. If it seems to be the hats, for example, try putting on a hat. If it seems to be the baby dolls, hold a doll out to the child.**

If a child plays eagerly and enthusiastically but is often on the verge of losing control . . .

> **. . . go to the same play area as this child while his or her play is appropriate. Play in some of the same ways as the child. Try to slow the pace, redirect, or just give a gentle touch before the child's behavior escalates.**

If a child is apt to run in the hallway on the way to the playground or bathroom . . .

> **. . . position yourself near the child. Anticipate the child's behavior. Ask the child to hold your hand, or ask the child a question.**

Your ideas:

Use praise and encouragement to help the child continue in an activity or a routine and to learn from his or her participation.

If a child repeatedly takes a book, flips the pages, and gets another book at the library corner and does the same thing . . .

> **. . . make a positive comment about the child's play and ask if the child can show you another way to use the book, or demonstrate another way and ask the child to do the same action.**

If a child usually tries to avoid cleaning up by immediately going to the next activity . . .

> **. . . just as cleanup time is ready to begin, position yourself near this child and start your cleanup song with the child's name.**

If a child is not an active participant during singing and other music activities . . .

> **. . . keep a subtle eye on the child. Whenever the child does an action or sings, give the child full eye contact and a smile.**

Your ideas:

Have a classmate model a way of participating.

If a child does not know how to select an activity or a game from the computer menu . . .

. . . pair the child with another child who is familiar with operating the computer, and let the peer show the child how to select an activity from the computer menu.

If a child is learning how to request food by signing during snack time . . .

. . . make sure that the child is sitting at the table with children who know the signs for snack items.

If a child is watching two children play with a new toy, and the child seems to be interested in the toy and wants to play with the two children . . .

. . . ask these two children to invite the child to join them and show him or her how to play with the toy.

Your ideas:

Pair the child with another child who can act as a helper.

If a child does not know when and where to line up during the transition to the playground . . .

. . . pair the child with another child who knows the routine and follows directions. Ask children to find their partner and hold their partner's hand when lining up.

If a child has difficulty lifting and putting the cover back on the sensory table during cleanup . . .

. . . ask other children to help. Make it a cooperative project.

If a child has trouble putting paint on sponges to make sponge prints . . .

. . . ask another child at his or her table to put paint on sponges for him or her, and then the child can make prints on the paper.

Your ideas:

Have peers use praise and encouragement.

If a child is learning to use words or signs to request food items at snack time . . .

. . . have another child hold the requested food (e.g., a plate of orange slices). The child then needs to request the oranges from the friend instead of an adult. This can be a nice change of routine: One child has the plate of fruit, another has the basket of crackers, another has the pitcher of juice, and everyone has to ask a friend.

If a child has difficulty with the table-top toys (e.g., LEGOs, puzzles, beads) and tends to give up easily when playing with them . . .

. . . pair the child with a classmate who is fun and talks a lot. Give the pair one set of toys that they need to play with together.

If a child always plays alone on the playground . . .

. . . identify a possible playmate who is fun and easygoing. Ask this child to play "follow the leader" with the other child. They can then take turns being the leader.

Your ideas:

Sequence turns to increase the likelihood of the child's participation.

If a child's hand strength is such that the child has difficulty during cooking activities that involve stirring or scooping . . .

. . . let the child take his or her turn after other children have stirred a bit or after another child has added liquid to the mixture. If the children are scooping out ice cream, let the child take a turn after the ice cream has melted a bit.

If a child is a reluctant talker during group activities . . .

. . . give the child a turn after the turn of another child who is particularly liked or is particularly talkative. This can give the child ideas about what to say or do.

If a child is learning to pour from a pitcher . . .

. . . let other children pour first so that the pitcher is not too full.

Your ideas:

Sequence activities within an activity or a learning center.

If a child needs more practice on a particular gross motor skill, such as walking on a balance beam . . .

> **. . . incorporate this skill into an obstacle course. Put a popular, fun, or noisy item after the more difficult one. For example, let the children hit a gong after they walk along the balance beam.**

If a child is working on matching . . .

> **. . . during the art activity of making collages, have the child's paper set up for matching; after the child completes matching the items, he or she can make the collage.**

If a child needs practice staying with the group during circle time . . .

> **. . . alternate active activities (e.g., songs with motions) with more passive activities (e.g., listening to stories).**

Your ideas:

Curriculum Modifications by Activity and Routine

This section provides some additional examples of ways to modify the curriculum to help children participate. These modifications are organized by the learning areas, planned activities, and routines often found in early childhood classrooms and centers. If a child in your classroom is having difficulty participating in a particular area or with a particular routine, find that section and look at the examples. These ideas should help spark your own thoughts about what will work in your classroom.

The first group of curriculum modifications addresses the learning centers that are common to many early childhood programs. These are art center, blocks, dramatic play, sensory table, book corner or library, computer center, and manipulatives or table-top toys.

The second group of curriculum modifications in this section addresses planned activities:

1. **Circle time:** Circle time or large-group meeting time offers an opportunity for children to come together and develop a sense of belonging. Circle times should allow children lots of opportunities for participating rather than waiting and watching. Activities should be meaningful to the children. Adjust the length of time to the children's developmental skills.
2. **Small group:** Small-group times are often adult-initiated activities that have preplanned learning goals. The same group of children meets with the same adult on a regular basis to explore, investigate, and learn new skills.
3. **Cooking:** Cooking increases the learning opportunities in the classroom. Children learn about food preparation and nutrition.
4. **Outdoor time:** Children should have time outdoors every day. In addition to physical activity, the outdoor environment can be viewed as an extension of the classroom, offering both additional and new learning opportunities.
5. **Music and movement:** Young children learn many important skills during music and movement activities. Some teachers incorporate music and movement into their circle times, others have a music center available during free-choice times, and others have a scheduled time for music and movement during the day.

A number of routine activities happen every day or several times a day in the early childhood classroom. These routines help form the structure of the day. They can also present valuable learning opportunities for children. The routines included in this book are arrival and departure, transitions, cleanup, snacks and meals, self-care routines, and rest time.

Art Center

Environmental Support

Alter the physical, social, and temporal environment to promote participation, engagement, and learning.

If a child messes up someone else's artwork or grabs things from a peer . . .

. . . provide physical boundaries for the art project by allowing children to do their art in a box lid or on a plastic tray.

If a child mouths art materials . . .

. . . use big art materials, such as big sponges to paint with instead of paint-brushes, and put all art materials in a bin with a "no eating" symbol on it.

Materials Adaptation

Modify materials so that the child can participate as independently as possible.

If a child has difficulty maintaining balance at the painting easel . . .

. . . cut the legs off of an easel (or shorten them), and place the easel on the table; the child can sit while painting.

If a child has difficulty grasping a sponge or does not like to get messy . . .

. . . glue a small block to the sponge so that the child can grasp the block instead of the sponge.

If a child sucks in instead of blowing out while blowing paint bubbles with a straw . . .

. . . cut a small notch out of the straw near the top; this prevents the child from sucking in.

Art Center

Activity Simplification

Simplify a complicated task by breaking it into smaller parts or by reducing the number of steps.

If a child is overwhelmed or frustrated with watercolor painting . . .

. . . break down the process into parts. Describe each step in clear single-word directions: "Water, paint, paper." Provide pictures of each step to make it even more clear.

If a child becomes frustrated with art or craft activities that require several skills (e.g., cutting, painting, printing name) . . .

. . . partially complete the steps so that the child only needs to demonstrate one skill and then is able to finish successfully. For example, for a project that requires children to cut out a house, write their name on it and paint it, or provide the child with a precut house with his or her name on it so that he or she only has to paint it to complete the activity.

Child Preferences

If the child is not taking advantage of the available opportunities, identify and integrate the child's preferences.

If a child does not play or remain engaged long at the art center . . .

. . . integrate a favorite item, activity, or person into the area. For example, if the child loves to play with cars and trucks, have some old cars and trucks at the art center. Let the children drive the cars through the paint and paint with the vehicles.

If a child does not choose the art center . . .

. . . pair the child with a preferred peer and let them go to the art center together.

Special Equipment

Use special or adaptive devices that allow a child to participate or increase a child's level of participation.

If a child doesn't yet have the strength or coordination to use a paint brush . . .

. . . try out other painting utensils. Visit the paint store or the art supply store, and consider roller brushes of various sizes, foam brushes, and so forth.

Adult Support

Have an adult intervene in an activity or a routine to support the child's participation and learning.

If a child repeats the same action over and over again, such as pounding the markers on the table . . .

. . . the adult can model how to do art another way while building on the child's action. For example, the adult could pound the marker in the shape of a circle or could pound two spots and draw a line between them.

Peer Support

Utilize peers to help the child learn important objectives.

If a child is unsure what to do when going to the art area . . .

. . . make sure the child goes to the area when other children are there to provide models of ways to use the materials.

If a child does not maintain proximity to peers . . .

. . . plan cooperative art activities with motivating supplies (e.g., squirter with paint, bubbles tinted with food coloring) so that the child needs to maintain proximity to peers while participating. This increases the opportunities for the child to learn by watching peers model appropriate ways to use the art materials.

Art Center

Invisible Support

Purposely arrange naturally occurring events within one activity.

If a child is unsure of how to complete or engage in an art activity . . .

. . . sequence turns so that another child, who can demonstrate how to start the activity, takes the first turn.

If a child has difficulty with cleanup after art activities . . .

. . . limit the number of transitions by having the child go to art just before snack time so that the child only needs to wash his or her hands once.

Your ideas:

Blocks

Environmental Support

Alter the physical, social, and temporal environment to promote participation, engagement, and learning.

If a child spreads blocks across the room . . .

. . . . establish boundaries for the block area with a rug or brightly colored tape.

If a child is unsure of what to do in the block area or does not progress in block play skills . . .

. . . display ideas around the block area, such as blueprints of buildings or photographs of simple block structures.

Materials Adaptation

Modify materials so that the child can pariticipate as independently as possible.

If a child with limited strength has difficulty using the wooden blocks . . .

. . . provide cardboard blocks. These can be made out of milk cartons and covered with Contact paper.

If a child with physical disabilities has trouble sitting on the floor and building . . .

. . . put a table in the block area. Let the child stand at the table or sit in an adapted chair at the table.

Child Preferences

If the child is not taking advantage of the available opportunities, identify and integrate the child's preferences.

If a child does not play or remain engaged long at the block area . . .

. . . integrate a favorite item, activity, or person. For example, if a child loves animals, place animal props in the block area. If the child likes to pound on things, place workbenches and toy hammers in the block area.

Blocks

Adult Support

Have an adult intervene in an activity or a routine to support the child's participation and learning.

If all of the child's building attempts fall down or get scattered and the child gets frustrated . . .

. . . join the child's play. Hand the blocks to the child one at a time to slow the child's pace.

If a child is playing cars and blocks in the block area, repeatedly bangs the blocks together, and makes lots of sounds like car engines . . .

. . . take a few blocks to build a road. Place a car on the "road" and imitate car engine noises while pushing the car along the road. Help the child use more blocks to make the road longer, and then push his or her car on the road and imitate the engine's sounds.

If a group of children are playing in the block area and some of these children get so excited that they may push and throw . . .

. . . join their play, make comments, and make eye contact. This can help prevent some problems.

Peer Support

Utilize peers to help the child learn important objectives.

If a child is trying to build a tower using interlocking blocks and cannot quite figure out how to fasten these blocks in a locked position, gets frustrated, and starts to throw the blocks . . .

. . . ask another child in the same area to show him or her how to put the blocks in a correct position so that they lock together.

If a child moves the blocks around the area but has difficulty building things . . .

. . . pair the child with a buddy who likes to build. Encourage the buddy to take turns as the children work on the same building.

Your ideas:

Dramatic Play

Environmental Support

Alter the physical, social, and temporal environment to promote participation, engagement, and learning.

If a child becomes overstimulated and does not engage in play . . .

. . . limit the amount of items in the dramatic play area to only a few things you know the child can be successful with. You can always add more later.

If a child does not engage in sociodramatic play . . .

. . . provide the child with a playscript. A playscript can be developed using either photos or drawings. The idea is to script a two- or three-part play sequence that the child can follow during play. For example, 1) get a pot, 2) put the pot on the stove, and 3) put the pot on the table and say, "Dinner's ready."

If a child perseverates on one play sequence or is disruptive in the dramatic play area . . .

. . . use items from the dramatic play area during circle time and small-group time to teach new ways to play. This can provide direction and structure for children who are usually disruptive and can expand a child's play skill repertoire.

Materials Adaptation

Modify materials so that the child can participate as independently as possible.

If a child uses a walker or wheelchair . . .

. . . make sure there is enough space in the classroom for the child to maneuver. Try it out yourself. You may need two tables in the area so that they are at varied heights.

If a child has difficulty gripping or handling tools . . .

. . . stock the housekeeping center with easy-to-grip spoons, forks, and handles. Build up handles with foam or tape. Full-size utensils may be easier to hold than child-size utensils.

If a child has difficulty fastening clothes . . .

. . . make sure the dress-up clothes are easy to put on and take off. Adapt with Velcro. Include items that are simpler to use, such as hats, sunglasses, or purses.

Child Preferences

If the child is not taking advantage of the available opportunities, identify and integrate the child's preferences.

If a child does not play or remain engaged long at the dramatic play area . . .

. . . develop a prop box that reflects the child's interests. For example, if a child loves trains, create a train station in the dramatic play area with a ticket booth, maps, and cardboard box trains.

. . . integrate favorite toys, activities, or people. For example, if the child likes the color yellow, place yellow dress-up clothes, yellow dishes, and so forth in the dramatic play area.

Adult Support

Have an adult intervene in an activity or routine to support the child's participation and learning.

If a child who is learning language skills plays with a tea set in the dramatic play area and he or she pretends to pour tea into a cup and drink it . . .

. . . bring a doll to the table. Pretend the doll is your guest, serve tea to the doll, and then begin a conversation with the doll.

If a child wanders in and out of the dramatic play area but never gets beyond trying one thing . . .

. . . join the child. Watch to see what the child looks at or does. Do the same thing, no matter how simple. Then, gradually take turns and expand on the child's play. For example, if the child looks in the mirror, you look in the mirror and say something.

Peer Support

Utilize peers to help the child learn important objectives.

If children are washing baby dolls in the dramatic play area and a child wants to wash the doll but has trouble removing the small clothes from the doll . . .

. . . ask another child to help him or her take off the baby doll's clothes, so the child can enjoy washing the baby doll.

Dramatic Play

If a child likes to go to the dramatic play area but often seems to get stuck after dressing a doll with clothes and shoes . . .

. . . invite children with more advanced play skills in the area. They can show the child what else the doll can wear (e.g., a hat, a purse) and what else the child can do with the doll (e.g., talk to the doll, walk the doll, have tea with the doll).

If a child does not often choose the dramatic play area . . .

. . . pair the child with a classmate who likes this area. Ask the classmate to take the child to the dramatic play area for a little while.

Invisible Support

Purposely arrange naturally occurring events within one activity.

If a child loses interest or always does the same thing in the housekeeping area . . .

. . . add props gradually and naturally. For example, add a suitcase to the housekeeping area. Put a few new articles of clothing in it.

. . . add props gradually and naturally to integrate themes. For example, add a large refrigerator box to the housekeeping area that can become a car to go to and from the house.

Your ideas:

Sensory Table

Environmental Support

Alter the physical, social, and temporal environment to promote participation, engagement, and learning.

If a child does not like to get dirty or get his or her hands messy . . .

. . . provide child-size gloves that the child can wear while playing in the area.

If a child loses interest or does not engage at the sensory table . . .

. . . place novel items in the table each week or hide small toys children can look for.

If a child always gets wet or dirty during play in the sensory table . . .

. . . have smocks near the sensory table so that children can put them on as they enter the area and do not need to leave the area to get a smock and then come back. This can also serve to limit the number of children in the area.

Materials Adaptation

Modify materials so that the child can participate as independently as possible.

If a child has difficulty grasping objects . . .

. . . provide easy-to-grasp tools, such as shovels, scoops, spoons, or tongs. If necessary, build up the handles with foam and tape.

If a child uses a walker or wheelchair and has difficulty reaching into a sturdy and strong table. . . .

. . . and the table is sturdy and strong, let the child sit in the table. You could also put the table on the floor, or give children plastic tubs for individual sensory tables.

If a child has difficulty seeing the sensory materials . . .

. . . make sure the materials (e.g., sand, water) contrast in color with the table and the toys. Dye the water with food coloring to see if that helps the child.

Sensory Table

Child Preferences

If the child is not taking advantage of the available opportunities, identify and integrate the child's preferences.

If a child does not play or remain long at the sensory table . . .

. . . integrate a favorite item. For example, if a child loves fish, place water in the table with plastic fish. If a child likes spinning things, provide sand toys that have spinning parts.

. . . integrate a favorite motor action. For example, if a child loves to pound, place plastic hammers on the sensory table with golf tees and let the child pound "nails" into the sand; or freeze plastic animals in water and then let children pound the ice block with hammers to loosen the animals.

. . . station a favorite adult or peer at the sensory table.

Peer Support

Utilize peers to help the child learn important objectives.

If a child is pouring sand into a bottle but he or she keeps tipping the bottle, gets frustrated, and starts to pour sand onto the floor . . .

. . . have another child stabilize the bottle on the sensory table so he or she can successfully pour sand into the bottle without tipping it over.

If a child is reluctant to play at the sensory table . . .

. . . pair the child with a classmate. Give the pair a toy to share. For example, give them one bucket and give each of them a scoop.

If a child does the same actions over and over again at the sensory table . . .

. . . encourage the child to join children who are playful, interactive, and have lots of ideas.

Invisible Support

Purposely arrange naturally occurring events within one activity.

If a child does the same thing over and over at the sensory table . . .

. . . add items gradually and naturally. For example, if the child fills and dumps with the containers, add spoons or shovels.

If a child loses interest in the sensory table . . .

. . . place a box or tub of new (or different) toys near the sensory table. Let the children "discover" the new toys.

Your ideas:

Book Corner

Environmental Support

Alter the physical, social, and temporal environment to promote participation, engagement, and learning.

If a child is distracted . . .

. . . carefully consider the arrangement of your book corner. It should be in a low-traffic area and near other quiet centers.

If a child is active and noisy in this area . . .

. . . carefully consider the materials that are available. Provide earphones for those who use CD/MP3 players, tablets, or other devices. Limit the number of children who can use the area at one time.

If a child never uses the area during free-choice time . . .

. . . use the book corner at other times of the day, as appropriate, to introduce the child to the area. For example, have the child's small group meet in the book corner.

Materials Adaptation

Modify materials so that the child can participate as independently as possible.

If a child has difficulty sitting on the floor . . .

. . . provide a child-size table and chair in the area for the child.

If a child has difficulty turning the pages . . .

. . . place bits of Styrofoam in the upper right-hand corner of the pages. It makes them easier to lift. You can also make or use cardboard books.

If a child is not yet interested in storybooks . . .

. . . include photograph albums with pictures of the children. Make photograph albums of field trips and class activities.

Activity Simplification

Simplify a complicated task by breaking it into smaller parts or by reducing the number of steps.

If a child has difficulty operating toys or equipment with multiple requirements (e.g., CD/MP3 player, activity boxes) . . .

. . . use green tape (for *start*) and red tape (for *stop*) on the buttons to show the steps. Or use numbers for multiple-step operations.

If a child does not have the fine motor skills to write but has something to say . . .

. . . include a magnetic board and letters as another way for the child to express him- or herself.

Child Preferences

If the child is not taking advantage of the available opportunities, identify and integrate the child's preferences.

If a child does not frequent or remain long at the book corner . . .

. . . integrate a favorite topic into the book selections. For example, if a child loves horses, place several horse books in the book corner. If a child has favorite books at home, place copies of these books in the book corner.

. . . integrate a favorite movement or motor action. For example, if a child loves to make noise, place some sound-producing books in the book corner.

. . . place toys that go along with certain books in the book corner. For example, offer *The Very Hungry Caterpillar* (Carle, 1969) and add some plastic fruits and vegetables and a caterpillar puppet. (Socks with eyes on them work great.)

Book Corner

Adult Support

Have an adult intervene in an activity or a routine to support the child's participation and learning.

If a child rarely chooses the book/library corner . . .

. . . station the child's favorite adult in the book corner.

If a child gets very loud or excited when listening to the audio books . . .

. . . have an adult join the child. The adult can use a gentle pat or touch to help the child control his or her excitement.

Peer Support

Utilize peers to help the child learn important objectives.

If a child flips through the books and quickly leaves the book corner . . .

. . . pair the child with a classmate. Have the classmate "read" a story. Then have them switch.

If a child has difficulty using and listening to the audio books . . .

. . . hook up two pairs of earphones to the CD/MP3 player, tablet, or other device. Have children listen to the book in pairs.

If a child is learning to talk, and he or she chooses to read books during free-choice time . . .

. . . encourage children to read stories to each other. The child can have more chances to observe how to tell a story and to practice talking.

Your ideas:

Computer Center

Environmental Support

Alter the physical, social, and temporal environment to promote participation, engagement, and learning.

If a child has difficulty waiting for a turn . . .

. . . have the children sign up on a dry-erase board or chalkboard for a turn. After a child finishes, he or she crosses off his or her name. Prewritten names on pieces of paper backed with Velcro can also be used to indicate a child's turn.

If a child wants to use the computer when it is not an option . . .

. . . indicate that the computer area is closed by covering each monitor with a large cloth or a piece of paper taped to the screen with a stop sign on it.

If a child has difficulty using the computer center independently . . .

. . . post picture directions at the center.

Special Equipment

Use special or adaptive devices that allow a child to participate or increase a child's level of participation.

If because of a sensory or physical disability a child is not able to use the hardware in your classroom . . .

. . . contact your local or state technology resource center for children and adults with special needs. You may be able to borrow adapted equipment that will work for the child. Look at an adaptive equipment catalog to help you make your own short-term solution.

Computer Center

Peer Support

Utilize peers to help the child learn important objectives.

If a child has difficulty with a new computer program . . .

. . . pair the child with a classmate who uses slower and more systematic strategies to figure out a new program.

If a child always chooses the computer and interacts with the computer to the exclusion of peer interaction . . .

. . . ensure that buddies use the computer together. Learn the child's favorite program and set up another play area with similar materials.

Your ideas:

Manipulatives

Environmental Support

Alter the physical, social, and temporal environment to promote participation, engagement, and learning.

If a child is easily distracted by the more active centers in the classroom . . .

. . . arrange the center to reduce distractions. Use L-shaped shelves. Place the manipulative center in a quiet part of the room.

If a child interferes with another child's materials at this center . . .

. . . use trays or box lids as individual workspaces.

Materials Adaptation

Modify materials so that the child can participate as independently as possible.

If a child has difficulty handling the string for bead stringing . . .

. . . glue dowels to a board. Use spools or blocks with holes drilled in them as beads. Have the child place the beads on the dowels.

If a child has difficulty handling puzzle pieces . . .

. . . provide a range of puzzle types. Glue spools or small blocks to the tops of puzzle pieces for handles.

If a child has difficulty handling game pieces, or game pieces keep scattering during the game . . .

. . . attach Velcro to both the play pieces and the game board. Or laminate the game board and pieces and use masking tape to keep things in place.

Manipulatives

Activity Simplification

Simplify a complicated task by breaking it into smaller parts or by reducing the number of steps.

If a child is interested in but overwhelmed by puzzles . . .

. . . help the child learn the steps: Spill out the pieces, turn the pieces right side up, start with pieces that form the edge, and so forth.

If a child is interested in but overwhelmed by sequencing or patterning activities . . .

. . . start the pattern, then let the child finish it.

Adult Support

Have an adult intervene in an activity or a routine to support the child's participation and learning.

If a child has difficulty taking a turn or following the rules for table games . . .

. . . join the children's play. Take turns with the children and use gentle coaching to help the children learn the rules.

If a child insists on selecting the most complex toy, gets frustrated, and throws it . . .

. . . join the child's play. Hand the pieces to the child one at a time, talk through strategies for doing the activity, or model asking for help.

Your ideas:

____

____

____

____

____

Circle Time

Environmental Support

Alter the physical, social, and temporal environment to promote participation, engagement, and learning.

If a child has difficulty keeping his or her hands to him- or herself during circle time . . .

. . . provide children with individual boundaries by having them sit on individual carpet squares.

If a child has difficulty attending to stories . . .

. . . be sure that everyone can see the storybook. Sometimes, children cannot see the book because they are seated too close or too far away. Select short stories, then gradually increase the length.

If a child has difficulty attending to rhymes or songs . . .

. . . use objects or puppets to act out rhymes or songs to make them more meaningful. This is especially helpful with students whose first language is not English.

Materials Adaptation

Modify materials so that the child can participate as independently as possible.

If a child is disinterested in circle-time activities and does not yet use verbal language . . .

. . . allow the child to choose a song, book, or fingerplay by pointing to a picture of the selection or by selecting a certain activity card.

If a child does not yet use verbal language and is disruptive or passive during songs and rhymes . . .

. . . provide the child objects or flannel pieces associated with the song or rhyme.

Circle Time

Activity Simplification

Simplify a complicated task by breaking it into smaller parts or by reducing the number of steps.

If a child leaves circle time or is disruptive when stories are read . . .

. . . read a story that is repetitive and has simple language (e.g., *Brown Bear, Brown Bear, What Do You See?* [Carle, 1967]; *The Napping House* [Wood, 2000]; *Go Away, Big Green Monster!* [Emberley, 1992]) every day for the week. As the child learns the story and begins to understand it, he or she will increase engagement. Other children will benefit because stories that are read repeatedly help children learn to read.

If a child has difficulty understanding stories . . .

. . . use objects or flannel board pieces that represent characters or objects in the story. The child may make connections between the physical objects and the story. This can be especially helpful for children whose first language is not English.

Child Preferences

If the child is not taking advantage of the available opportunities, identify and integrate the child's preferences.

If a child has a tantrum and tries to leave large-group times such as circle time . . .

. . . let the child hold a favorite quiet toy (e.g., teddy bear, baby doll). Give him or her the toy at the beginning of group time.

If a child is not willing to go to or participate during circle time . . .

. . . begin circle time with a favorite activity or toy. For example, when only a few children are at circle time, begin blowing bubbles for them while saying, "Tommy is at circle. He's playing with bubbles." Other activities include giving children a squirt of lotion, spraying water, playing a favorite movement song, or giving children a turn with a favorite toy, such as a whirligig. As soon as the target child arrives at circle time, reinforce him or her with a turn.

If a child is hesitant to go to circle time . . .

. . . have a favorite person (child or adult) sit next to an empty carpet square so that the child knows he or she can be near a favorite person as soon as he or she sits at circle time.

Special Equipment

Use special or adaptive devices that allow a child to participate or increase a child's level of participation.

If a child has difficulty maintaining trunk stability while sitting at circle time . . .

. . . allow the child to sit in a cube chair so that he or she is still at the same height as the other children but is in a more stable position. Once a child's trunk and hips are stabilized, the child can increase active participation because he or she will expend less energy sitting and more energy moving his or her arms and hands to the songs and fingerplays.

Adult Support

Have an adult intervene in an activity or a routine to support the child's participation and learning.

If a child does not participate in circle-time activities, such as movements to songs or fingerplays . . .

. . . have an adult sit behind the child and provide hand-over-hand assistance to prompt the child to do the movements. As the child becomes more independent, the adult should gradually decrease his or her assistance.

If a child is unsure of what to do during circle-time activities . . .

. . . have an adult sit next to the child and model exaggerated movements while praising and encouraging the child as he or she approximates the movements.

Peer Support

Utilize peers to help the child learn important objectives.

If a child is asked to choose the picture that shows today's weather and put it on the weather board but he or she does not know which one to pick . . .

. . . ask a peer to pick a picture and give it to the child so that the child can still put the picture on the board.

Circle Time

If children are asked to choose an animal whose name has the same first letter as theirs (e.g., *elephant* for *Eric*) and pretend to be that animal during the zoo activity at circle time but one child cannot think of any animals that he or she can pretend to be . . .

. . . ask other children to suggest animals that have the same first letter as the child's name. Let the child decide which animal he or she wants to pretend to be.

If the teacher passes a "magic bag" around during circle time and has each child pick one thing from the bag without looking but one child does not want to put his or her hand into the bag . . .

. . . ask the child's buddy to pick one thing from the bag for the child. The child can hold it while the other children pick items.

Invisible Support

Purposely arrange naturally occurring events within one activity.

If a child often gives nonsensical or inappropriate responses to circle-time questions . . .

. . . call on a child who will model an appropriate response just before calling on that particular child.

If a child is unsure of what to do at circle time . . .

. . . seat the child between and across from peers who will consistently model appropriate actions.

Your ideas:

____

____

____

____

____

Small Group

Environmental Support

Alter the physical, social, and temporal environment to promote participation, engagement, and learning.

If a child grabs objects from others . . .

. . . add physical structure to the activity by putting the child's project on a plastic tray or in a cardboard box lid. This way, the child has a reminder of which items are his or hers and are relevant to the project.

If a child has difficulty making the transition to small-group time . . .

. . . assign seats at the small-group table. Post the child's name on the table or on his or her chair. This ensures that children know exactly where they need to sit at small-group time and eliminates transition chaos. Or give the child a name card to take to small-group time.

If a child has difficulty following directions . . .

. . . present only one step with the corresponding item at a time. Present another step only after he or she has completed the first.

Materials Adaptation

Modify materials so that the child can participate as independently as possible.

If a child is matching word cards to pictures of objects but the child's arm movements move the cards out of their correct places . . .

. . . put Velcro on the back of the cards and the pictures. Let the child attach the cards and the pictures to a board.

If the table is too high for the child . . .

. . . attach a foam board or cushion to the child's seat by using Velcro or tape.

If a child has difficulty holding a pencil . . .

. . . wrap the pencil with tape so that it becomes bigger and easier for the child to hold.

Small Group

Activity Simplification

Simplify a complicated task by breaking it into smaller parts or by reducing the number of steps.

If a child has difficulty with puzzles or games that have lots of pieces . . .

. . . hand the pieces to the child one by one, or start with a completed puzzle and gradually increase the number of the pieces taken out.

If a child is overwhelmed by the project the group is working on . . .

. . . make picture cards to illustrate the steps or parts of the activity.

Child Preferences

If the child is not taking advantage of the available opportunities, identify and integrate the child's preferences.

If a child has a tantrum and tries to leave the small group . . .

. . . let the child hold a favorite quiet toy or a material that will be used during the activity. Give the child the toy before the activity begins.

If a child is not willing to go to or participate at small group . . .

. . . integrate a favorite item into the activity. For example, if a child loves trains, have the child run a toy train through paint to create his or her artwork instead of using a paintbrush.

If a child finishes the activity quickly and then wants to leave . . .

. . . create "finished boxes" with motivating items inside that the child can use only after he or she finishes small group and remains at the small-group table.

Adult Support

Have an adult intervene in an activity or a routine to support the child's participation and learning.

If a child seems to be confused by the steps involved in a cutting and pasting activity and does not know where to start . . .

. . . have an adult sit beside the child and show him or her how to cut out a shape and glue it to the paper without telling him or her directly.

If a child appears to be getting frustrated in the activity . . .

. . . provide encouragement by taking turns with the child.

Peer Support

Utilize peers to help the child learn important objectives.

If a child has difficulty putting the last few pieces of a puzzle in the correct places . . .

. . . let another child who has put the puzzle together successfully tell or give clues to the child about where the pieces go.

If a child has difficulty opening a jar to get playdough or other materials out . . .

. . . pair the child with another child so that the partner can hold the bottom of the container firmly on the table while the child takes off the cover.

If a child with fine motor difficulties becomes frustrated while stringing beads because the beads keep falling out of the child's hands when he or she tries to hold the string in one hand and the bead in the other hand . . .

. . . pair the child with another child, and ask the partner to hold the beads for him or her so that the target child can focus on putting the string through the beads. Or, ask the pair to figure out who will do which part of the task.

Small Group

Invisible Support

Purposely arrange naturally occurring events within one activity.

If a child spends most of small-group time standing or squirming in the chair . . .

. . . move the small group to an area of the room where sitting at the table is not required.

If a child has difficulty understanding the teacher's verbal directions . . .

. . . give the child a turn immediately after a child who is successful.

Your ideas:

Cooking

Environmental Support

Alter the physical, social, and temporal environment to promote participation, engagement, and learning.

If a child has difficulty waiting for a turn . . .

. . . do cooking activities during small-group time instead of with the whole class. Or, do cooking activities on days when you have additional adults in the classroom and can form more than one cooking group.

If a child has difficulty following verbal directions . . .

. . . illustrate the cooking directions by using picture cards.

If a child tends to get into "elbow fights" during cooking . . .

. . . place the child at the end of the table, where he or she has more room.

Materials Adaptation

Modify materials so that the child can participate as independently as possible.

If a child has difficulty stabilizing or holding equipment . . .

. . . use nonskid materials on the table. Let the child stand if this helps.

Cooking

Activity Simplification

Simplify a complicated task by breaking it into smaller parts or by reducing the number of steps.

If a child has difficulty using the cooking gadgets . . .

. . . have the children work in small groups. Each group contributes to the whole cooking project. For example, one group washes the vegetables, one group peels them, and one group cuts them. Have this child work in the vegetable-washing group.

If a child has difficulty doing all the steps . . .

. . . set up the cooking activity like an assembly line and have the children each do one important step.

Your ideas:

Outdoor Time

Materials Adaptation

Modify materials so that the child can participate as independently as possible.

If a child cannot reach the pedals on a tricycle or Big Wheel . . .

. . . build up the pedals with blocks of wood taped to the pedals.

Child Preferences

If the child is not taking advantage of the available opportunities, identify and integrate the child's preferences.

If a child does not participate . . .

. . . do not limit the outdoor space to large-muscle activities. Add easels and paint; musical instruments; or a picnic table and board games.

If a child does not participate in certain areas of the playground . . .

. . . assign a favorite adult to that area.

If a child wants to play ball games but does not understand taking turns or other rules . . .

. . . teach ball games during the child's small-group time.

Adult Support

Have an adult intervene in an activity or a routine to support the child's participation and learning.

If a child does the same thing day after day . . .

. . . join the child's play, but bring something new with you.

If a child runs excitedly and often gets in the way of the swings and slides . . .

. . . make a running track with tape or chalk. Organize a "track meet" or other running event.

Outdoor Time

Peer Support

Utilize peers to help the child learn important objectives.

If a child is trying to pull a wagon but it is too heavy for him or her . . .

. . . ask another child to help the target child so that together they are able to move the wagon.

If a child has vision problems and has difficulty going through the obstacle course . . .

. . . pair the child with another child who has good vision and gross motor skills. Let the children figure out the best way to do the obstacle course.

If a child is reluctant to try the slide or another piece of equipment . . .

. . . ask a classmate to invite the child to join him or her on the equipment.

Your ideas:

Music and Movement

Child Preferences

If the child is not taking advantage of the available opportunities, identify and integrate the child's preferences.

If a child does not participate . . .

. . . incorporate a favorite toy into the activity. For example, if a child likes trucks, have the children roll trucks back and forth in time to the music.

. . . have the children participate in groups of two or three. Assign this child to a group that includes a favorite peer or adult.

If a child does not do the hand motions in fingerplays . . .

. . . have the children look at themselves in mirrors while doing the activity. (Use the mirrors from the dress-up area.)

Adult Support

Have an adult intervene in an activity or a routine to support the child's participation and learning.

If a child does not participate actively . . .

. . . describe what the child is doing. Introduce new words, such as *bouncy* or *smooth*.

If a child does not try new movements or actions . . .

. . . imitate the child. Take turns. Eventually introduce a new movement and see if the child imitates you.

Music and Movement

Invisible Support

Purposely arrange naturally occurring events within one activity.

If a child does not participate during large-group music and movement activities . . .

. . . incorporate music and movement into other activities. For example, have the child hop or take "giant steps" to the next activity. Include several of these activities during the day.

If a child is not interested in music activities . . .

. . . have the children make their own musical instruments (e.g., drums, maracas, tambourines) during art or small-group time. The child may be more interested in music if he or she gets to play his or her own instrument.

Your ideas:

Arrival and Departure

Environmental Support

Alter the physical, social, and temporal environment to promote participation, engagement, and learning.

If a child struggles or balks when entering the classroom . . .

. . . have the children's name cards or pictures available outside the classroom. Let the child take his or her name or picture card into the classroom and place it on a large picture of the school. At end of the day, reverse the process.

If a child has difficulty getting settled into the daily routine . . .

. . . place a picture card in the child's cubby. The picture card indicates the child's first task of the day (e.g., going to the block area).

If a child wanders or dawdles on the way to the bus at the end of the day . . .

. . . give the child a picture symbol or a "bus pass" to take to the bus driver.

Activity Simplification

Simplify a complicated task by breaking it into smaller parts or by reducing the number of steps.

If a child acts out while waiting for the other children to get ready to leave . . .

. . . reduce waiting time. Arrange for an adult to supervise departure as soon as a few children are ready to leave.

If a child takes an excessive amount of time to complete the various departure tasks . . .

. . . decide which tasks are most important. Have the child do these independently. Help with the others. Gradually increase the child's responsibility for all departure tasks.

Arrival and Departure

Child Preferences

If the child is not taking advantage of the available opportunities, identify and integrate the child's preferences.

If a child wanders or dawdles at departure time . . .

. . . help the child write a short note about his or her favorite activity that day. Have the child carry it home.

If a child's transition from the bus or car to the classroom is slow . . .

. . . have outdoor time as the first activity if possible.

Your ideas:

Transitions

Environmental Support

Alter the physical, social, and temporal environment to promote participation, engagement, and learning.

If a child tends to stay in one area and does not seem to explore other areas . . .

. . . set a timer for the child. When the timer beeps, the child goes to another area so that he or she can explore all the areas.

If a child does not seem to know where he or she is going to sit before circle time begins . . .

. . . put his or her name on a mat and arrange it before the activity starts. If the child does not yet identify his or her name, give the child another name card and have him or her match it to the one on the mat.

If a child has a hard time following classroom routines and does not seem to know what is going to happen in the classroom . . .

. . . use a picture schedule. Let the child turn over the card after each activity is finished.

If a child continues to have difficulty following directions during transitions . . .

. . . give a silly transition cue. For example, have the child walk sideways to the bathroom.

Child Preferences

If the child is not taking advantage of the available opportunities, identify and integrate the child's preferences.

If a child is wandering around in the classroom while the other children are lining up at the door to go outside . . .

. . . let the child's favorite person (a teacher or a peer) tell him or her to come to the line and hold hands while the child is waiting or walking to the playground.

If a child has difficulty making transitions from activity to activity . . .

. . . think of a favorite toy or activity the child likes to do, and then find or draw a picture of it. Cut the picture into as many pieces as there are transitions. Each time the child successfully makes a transition, give the child a piece of the puzzle. When the child puts all of the pieces together, he or she gets to do that activity or play with that toy.

Transitions

Adult Support

Have an adult intervene in an activity or a routine to support the child's participation and learning.

If a child does not seem to know what to do during the transition from small-group activity to free-choice time . . .

. . . near the end of the small-group activity, tell the child what he or she can do after he or she finishes. For example, you might say, "When you finish that, you can pick an area where you want to go. What areas do you want to play in? We have blocks, books . . . "

If a child seems surprised at or hurried during transitions . . .

. . . give the child an individualized warning about 5 minutes before the transition.

If a child does not seem to know what to do during a transition . . .

. . . listen to your own instructions. Be sure that they are clear, specific, and consistent.

Peer Support

Utilize peers to help the child learn important objectives.

If a child does not seem to know what to do and where to go during transitions . . .

. . . pair the child with another child who knows the routine well.

If during the transition from circle time to small-group time children are required to move their photo and name tag from the circle-time board to the small-group board at their table, and one child has difficulty with this concept . . .

. . . let some of the other children who know the routine choose which table they want to go to. Have them take their photos to the small-group board before you call on the target child, so the child can see what he or she needs to do several times before he or she actually does it.

If a child does not lie down on his or her mat during the transition to rest time and instead wanders around the classroom . . .

. . . make sure the other children lie down first before asking the target child to lie down.

Your ideas:

Cleanup

Environmental Support

Alter the physical, social, and temporal environment to promote participation, engagement, and learning.

If a child becomes confused and distracted during cleanup time . . .

. . . outline toys, blocks, and other classroom objects on shelves or place photos on shelves so children know where the toys go.

If a child becomes frustrated during cleanup time . . .

. . . use big buckets or bins that are labeled for blocks, toys, and so forth so that the child has a clear idea of where toys belong.

If a child refuses to clean up . . .

. . . make cleanup tickets. Draw pictures or use photographs of various areas in the classroom and allow a child to pick a card or ticket. The card the child picks is where he or she cleans up. When the child is done, he or she gives the card back as a ticket to go to the next activity.

Adult Support

Have an adult intervene in an activity or a routine to support the child's participation and learning.

If a child does not know where the big blocks go when cleaning up the block area . . .

. . . pick up a few blocks and put them where they belong on the shelves to show the child where to put them.

If a child wants to help clean up the table after snack time but does not know exactly what to do . . .

. . . put a couple of plates in the basket to give the child an idea of where to start.

If a child is trying to wash paint off his or her hands without using soap . . .

. . . put paint on your hands, too. Then, put some soap on your hands and rub them together to show the child how to get the paint off.

Peer Support

Utilize peers to help the child learn important objectives.

If a child is cleaning tables after snack and cannot figure out how to squirt soap on the table before wiping it . . .

. . . pair the child with another child so that one child can squirt the soap on the table and the other child can wipe the table clean.

If a child often does not wash his or her hands thoroughly after painting . . .

. . . pair the child with another child who usually cleans his or her hands well. Ask children to check their partner's hands after washing them.

If a child does not help at cleanup time . . .

. . . assign two children to a task. For example, one child holds the bin, and another gathers the cups and puts them in.

Your ideas:

Snacks and Meals

Child Preferences

If the child is not taking advantage of the available opportunities, identify and integrate the child's preferences.

If a child eats very little or will not try new things . . .

. . . have a favorite adult eat with the children at this child's table.

. . . incorporate child participation into snack or meal preparation. This can be something simple, such as watching cheese melt on toast, making the juice, or stirring the yogurt into the fruit salad.

If a child is learning to use a napkin . . .

. . . use napkins that are the child's favorite color or that have pictures of the child's favorite things on them.

Peer Support

Utilize peers to help the child learn important objectives.

If a child is learning how to use a spoon properly . . .

. . . make sure that the child is sitting at the table with other children who can use a spoon appropriately so that the target child can see how others use spoons during snack time.

If a child is learning to use signs to request something . . .

. . . ask another child, who also signs, what he or she wants before giving him or her more food so that the target child can have a chance to observe a peer using signs to make a request.

If a child has difficulty pouring juice from a pitcher . . .

. . . ask another child at the same table to pour juice for him or her. Give the target child another job.

Your ideas:

Self-Care Routines

Environmental Support

Alter the physical, social, and temporal environment to promote participation, engagement, and learning.

If a child is learning all the steps of toileting or hand washing . . .

. . . put pictures next to the toilet or washbasin that illustrate the steps.

If a child forgets to flush the toilet . . .

. . . put brightly colored tape on the handle as a reminder. Change the tape as needed.

Materials Adaptation

Modify materials so that the child can participate as independently as possible.

If a child cannot reach or operate the paper towel dispenser . . .

. . . place a basket of single paper towels on the counter.

If a child is learning to zip a jacket . . .

. . . enlarge the tab of the zipper by adding a ring or other zipper pull.

Your ideas:

Rest Time

Child Preferences

If the child is not taking advantage of the available opportunities, identify and integrate the child's preferences.

If a child is restless and loud . . .

. . . let the child hold a favorite quiet toy (e.g., teddy bear, baby doll).

. . . have quiet books that children really enjoy in a basket that is available only at rest time. Even if the child does not nap, he or she can look at "special books" quietly.

. . . allow the child to listen to recorded storybooks or soothing music with headphones, contingent on his or her remaining on the mat.

If a child is not willing to lie down for naptime . . .

. . . let the child choose where he or she wants to lie down. Offer a choice, such as "Do you want to sleep on the red mat or the blue mat?"

Adult Support

Have an adult intervene an activity or a routine to support the child's participation and learning.

If a child wanders around the classroom . . .

. . . go to the rest area. Help children settle down by rubbing their backs, talking quietly, or providing books or stuffed animals.

Rest Time

Peer Support

Utilize peers to help the child learn important objectives.

If a child does not lie down on his or her mat . . .

. . . make sure that some of the other children lie down first in the rest area. When the child sees other children lying down quietly in the rest area, he or she may want to do what his or her peers are doing.

If a child is learning how to put his or her things away after rest time . . .

. . . pair the child with a peer who knows this routine. Have them help each other.

Your ideas:

SUMMARY

This chapter provides many examples of ways to modify or adapt learning activities, materials, or routines so that the individual child will actively participate in the early learning environment. It is assumed that teachers will plan lessons and materials that are interesting and appropriately challenging for all of the children in the group. Drawing on UDL principles, teachers may already use some of these strategies to help all children access the learning activities and environment. In this chapter, the strategies are used to help the individual child. By helping each child participate in a meaningful way with the activities and materials, teachers help children gain access to even more learning possibilities. This active or meaningful participation in the learning activities, interactions, and routines is sometimes called *engagement.* Increased engagement is associated with increased learning. Strategies that facilitate children's engagement are considered recommended practices in the field (Sandall, Hemmeter, Smith, & McLean, 2005). CMs can be powerful teaching strategies when planned and used intentionally. That is, teachers must be aware of individual children's needs and interests and have the ability to identify and use appropriate individualized supports that lead to positive outcomes for individual children. In our own work with early childhood teachers, we find that teachers quickly learn new CMs and report that they are easy to use in their classrooms and that, many times, such simple adjustments result in increased participation (Horn, Lieber, Sandall, Schwartz, & Wolery, 2001). However, if CMs are not sufficient to help a child participate or become engaged, it will be necessary to provide that child with more instructional support.

Chapter 6

Embedded Learning Opportunities

Early childhood teachers use embedded learning opportunities (ELOs) to create short, intentional teaching episodes within ongoing activities and routines. The teaching episodes focus on a child's individual learning objectives and are embedded within activities and routines; the instructional component is planned ahead of time.

ELOs can be used when the child shows interest in ongoing classroom activities and when there is a good match between the activity or routine and the child's learning objective. Using ELOs has a number of benefits. First, because existing activities and routines are used, this strategy should not require big changes to the classroom. Second, a teacher can take advantage of a child's interests and preferences, which should enhance the child's motivation to participate and learn. Third, because the teaching takes place in the natural setting of the classroom, the child's ability to use the newly learned skill by him- or herself is increased. And fourth, if the teacher plans to provide ELOs several times during the day and during different activities, the child's ability to use the skill in a variety of situations is also encouraged.

ELO refers to the particular feature of embedding instruction. The use of ELOs is based on the assumption that the teacher and team are already using a high-quality curriculum and their knowledge of appropriate standards or benchmarks to guide their planning of engaging activities. Furthermore, these activities are intended to help *all* children learn valued concepts and skills. The reason for using ELOs is that some children require guidance to take advantage of the learning opportunities within these activities, so the teacher and team plan teaching episodes to enable these children to more fully engage in activities and achieve their individualized objectives.

When planning and implementing ELOs, teachers and teams use instructional strategies that are likely to be effective, such as prompting and reinforcement. They use these strategies frequently so that the child learns the identified objective. Chapter 7 provides a discussion of these instructional strategies

One of Samisha's learning objectives focused on increasing her cooperative play skills with peers. One of the ways Gia and David, Samisha's teachers, decided to work on this was to embed planned teaching and learning opportunities in the classroom's free-choice time. The classroom features a learning center where the children can play with board games, such as Lotto. During free-choice time, Gia and David planned to invite Samisha to the table game center when other children who were more skilled players would be there. David then used prompts and encouragement to help Samisha learn the game and play cooperatively with her peers.

In this example, instead of setting up a special or separate time for Samisha to learn and practice cooperative play skills, her teachers did some extra planning so that they could embed the necessary instruction (in this case, using systematic prompting and encouragement) within the ongoing free-choice activities.

Just as teachers use ELOs to create short teaching episodes in their classrooms, families and other caregivers can use ELOs to increase teaching and learning opportunities within activities and daily routines at home or in the child care setting. The many activities and settings that make up the daily life of the family or the child care home or center are the sources and contexts in which learning opportunities are embedded.

One of Mateo's learning objectives is to use approximations of three to five single words. His visiting early interventionist, Kate, and Mateo's parents identified diapering, snacks and meals, and book reading as times in their daily routines to embed teaching. They chose a few words to focus on such as up, more, and book. During the routines, Mateo's parents modeled the words and used wait time, or an extra pause, to give him time to try to use his words. When he made an attempt, they repeated his vocalizations, smiled, and said the word again. Then, Kate worked with Dara at the family child care home to identify daily routines to use in the same way. They selected diapering, snacks and meals, going outside, and greeting Dad at the end of the day, and Dara began using modeling and wait time to help Mateo use words.

In this example, instead of trying to find special teaching times during their busy days, Mateo's parents and his child care provider reviewed their daily activities and found times when they could insert planned instruction throughout the day.

THE BASIC STEPS

Using ELOs sounds like a natural thing to do. However, teachers must plan very carefully to ensure that during ELOs, children with disabilities or other special needs are able to adequately practice their skills. Seven basic steps are necessary for planning and implementing ELOs:

1. Clarify the learning objective, and determine the criterion.
2. Gather baseline information to determine the child's current level of performance.
3. Use an activity matrix to select activities, learning centers, or routines in which instruction can reasonably be embedded. (See Chapter 4 for an example.)
4. Design the instructional interaction, and write it on a planning form. You can use an ELO-at-a-Glance (provided in Appendix A), which tells exactly what will happen during a teaching episode (adapted from McCormick & Feeney's "IEP-at-a-Glance" [1995]).
5. Implement the instruction as planned, remembering these tips:
   - Give clear instructions.
   - Let the child respond.
   - Provide feedback.
6. Keep track of the opportunities provided.
7. Periodically check to find out if the child has achieved the objective.

Drew was learning to follow teacher-given instructions. His learning objective stated that during the typical classroom day, Drew would respond to the first request to begin or complete activities. He would respond to at least 80% of first requests and would do so for 2 days in a row. After completing the Child Assessment Worksheet and examining the daily schedule, Drew's teacher and team decided that they would work on part of this objective during transitions from activity to activity. Drew's teacher, Jennie, and her assistant, Marlene, took a couple of days to observe his current performance at following instructions. They made a simple chart listing each transition and the instructions they would give Drew for the transition (e.g., "Time for circle," "Go to small group with Jennie"). They left a place to write "yes" or "no" after each instruction to record whether Drew follows the instruction on the first request. They collected information for 2 days and found out that Drew always needs more than one instruction except when it is time to go outside.

Jennie and Marlene talked about the best way to teach Drew to follow instructions. They decided to use a visual or picture prompt with him to help him better understand the direction. Look at Drew's Child Assessment Worksheet and Child Activity Matrix in Chapter 4 to review the planning done by his team.

Identifying the opportunities for learning is not enough. Next, Jennie, with help from the team, discussed and wrote a plan for Drew (see Figure 6.1).

This plan, called an ELO-at-a-Glance, tells what will happen during a teaching episode. Good teaching includes 1) a careful description of the expected child behavior (i.e., the objective), 2) what the teacher or other adult will do before this

ELO-at-a-Glance

Date: 1/07

Team members: Jennie (teacher) Marlene (assistant)

Child's name: Drew

Routines: Transitions

Objective: When shown a picture and given an instruction to start an activity, Drew will follow the instruction the first time it is given. He will do this 80% of the time, 2 days in a row.

What are you going to do? Show Drew the picture.

What are you going to say? "Drew, go to circle."

How will you respond? If Drew follows the instruction, praise and remind him of what he just did. If not, show picture, repeat instruction, and physically assist him.

What materials do you need? Pictures or photos of

Circle time	Drew's small group	Each play area	Bus
Soap dispenser	Juice and cookies	Slide and tricycle	

How many opportunities will you provide each day?

(Use Drew's transition chart to track progress)

Monday	Tuesday	Wednesday	Thursday	Friday
10	10	10	10	10

Figure 6.1. An ELO-at-a-Glance for Drew. (*Source:* Horn, Lieber, Li, Sandall, & Schwartz, 2000.)

behavior, and 3) what the teacher or other adult will do after the child's behavior. Drew's ELO-at-a-Glance shows all of these parts. In addition, the form tells the teacher about any materials he or she may need or any changes he or she may need to make to the typical activity in order to embed instruction. For Drew, Jennie needed pictures that will tell him what to do next. For example, she or Marlene will show Drew a picture of children at circle time and say, "Drew, go to circle." Before snack, she or Marlene will show Drew a picture of the soap dispenser and say, "Drew, it's time to wash hands," and so forth. See Figure 4.7 to see how ELOs appear on the activity matrix.

Pairing the ELO-at-a-Glance with the Evaluation Worksheet to collect information is helpful in determining if the ELO strategy is effective. Information can be collected in many ways. (These are described in Chapter 4.)

Information about a child's progress is meaningful only if the teachers have actually embedded the instruction. Sometimes, it is necessary to keep track of the adults' behavior to make sure that planned instruction occurs. The space at the bottom of the ELO-at-a-Glance can be used for this purpose. Part of the team's planning should be to decide how many opportunities to provide each day. One is not enough; the team should try for 10 or more. Teachers simply tally each time they provide an opportunity. In addition, teams should develop data collection systems to monitor the child's performance.

Drew's example illustrates how to use an ELO to help a child learn a skill that is best acquired within the context of classroom routines. The next example shows how to embed learning opportunities within free-choice time. In many early childhood classrooms, free-choice time, or learning center time, accounts for a significant portion of the classroom day. Thus, it is prime time for teaching and learning. It is not unusual for a young child with disabilities to have difficulty during free-choice time. Sometimes, a child does not have adequate social, language, or toy skills to participate during this time. Another child might have difficulty maintaining attention to the activities and does not grasp the concept or skill as the teacher might expect.

Samisha's learning objective states that during play times, Samisha will join her peers in play and maintain play with them for 10 minutes or more in cooperative play activities. She will demonstrate this in four different play areas. Samisha's teachers, Gia and David, completed the Child Assessment Worksheet, examined their daily schedule, and observed and took notes on Samisha's play during free-choice time (see Figure 6.2).

They noted that Samisha can take part in cooperative play in the dramatic play area but only if she initiates the story line. Even then, her cooperative play lasts only a couple of minutes. Gia and David also noted that Samisha has started to watch other children play games in the table game center.

One of the important considerations for Samisha's teachers is that there are six children with disabilities in this classroom, and many of the children have objectives that could be embedded during free-choice time. Gia and David need to be creative and realistic about how to use their time and resources. They decided to embed instruction on cooperative play at the table game center. Once Samisha is successful, they will work on this objective in other play areas. The current plan

Child Assessment Worksheet

Date: 1/17

Teacher's name: Gia Child's name: Samisha

Classroom activities	Classroom expectations	Child's level of performance
Arrival	Stay with class when walking to classroom. Walk independently	Strength ____ Average ____ Area of concern X
Circle time	Sit on own mat. Participate in music and movement games. Participate in literacy and numeracy activities.	Strength ____ Average X Area of concern ____
Small-group time	Stay at table. Participate in art and other small-group activities. Contribute questions and answers related to planned lesson.	Strength ____ Average X Area of concern ____
Free-choice time	Play independently. Play cooperatively with other children. Share and take turns. Explore all learning centers during the week.	Strength ____ Average ____ Area of concern X

(continued)

Child Assessment Worksheet

(continued)

Date: 1/17

Teacher's name: Gia   Child's name: Samisha

Classroom activities	Classroom expectations	Child's level of performance
Cleanup time	Clean area promptly when asked. Replace materials to shelves.	Strength ___ Average X Area of concern ___
Snack time	Stay at table. Eat snack. Talk with other children and pass items when asked.	Strength ___ Average X Area of concern ___
Outdoor time	Play on equipment in the playground. Play independently and with other children.	Strength ___ Average ___ Area of concern X
Transitions	Follow instructions. Stay with group.	Strength ___ Average X Area of concern ___

Figure 6.2. A Child Assessment Worksheet for Samisha.

means that one adult will work with three or four children. The structure of the game and systematic use of prompting will help Samisha learn to play with the other children. The teachers developed an ELO-at-a-Glance for Samisha (see Figure 6.3).

To maximize their time and resources, Gia and David could decide to use this same activity during free-choice time to embed instruction for another child in the class. Joey is one of Samisha's classmates. He also likes to play at the game table. This could be a prime time for the teacher (who is already there) to embed instruction on one of Joey's objectives: Joey will release a handheld object onto or into a larger target with either hand. The teachers select the game's playing pieces with Joey in mind and then use the slight minimal assistance he needs to help him place the playing piece on the appropriate section of the board game.

TIPS FOR CONSTRUCTING EMBEDDED LEARNING OPPORTUNITIES

Consulting ECSE teachers find the ELO approach and the planning forms useful in their work with community-based teachers. Once a teacher learns the approach and how to use the forms, the approach can be easily transferred to other children and their objectives. However, sometimes the community-based teacher believes that the child needs highly specialized one-to-one time with the consulting teacher. Other times, the IFSP or IEP is written in a way that makes it difficult to translate the child's goals and objectives to functional classroom behaviors. Following are some guidelines that may be helpful in these situations.

Tailoring the Learning Objective for the Preschool Classroom

It is important to remember that learning objectives are not the same thing as activities. Likewise, planning an activity is not the same as providing instruction (see Giangreco, Dennis, Edelman, & Cloninger, 1994). Community-based teachers are often skilled at planning interesting, fun activities for groups of young children; however, in an inclusive classroom, they may not be as experienced at ensuring that an individual child's objective is embedded and that sufficient instruction is provided. For example, a child may have several learning objectives aimed at skills such as reaching, grasping, making a request, or comprehending people's names. These objectives are not activities. They are skills that children are expected to use during genuine activities to participate more effectively in those activities. The teacher's job is to teach the child to do those skills and to use them during genuine activities. Just presenting the activities is not enough; teaching must also occur.

Sometimes, IFSP or IEP objectives are written in ways that may actually limit the potential for embedding the objective within genuine classroom activities. For example, a child's IEP objective may state, "Given the cue, 'Put the puzzle together' when presented with a three- to five-piece interlocking puzzle, Annie will disassemble the pieces and then put the puzzle back together on at least 80% of the response opportunities." This may lead a teacher to implement instruction on the objective by seating the child at a table and providing the child with repeated opportunities with a selected set of puzzles. This is unlikely to occur in an active, play-based classroom, and it may not be very motivating for the child. It is more likely that children

ELO-at-a-Glance

Date: 1/17

Team members: Gia (teacher) David (assistant)

Child's name: Samisha

Routines: Free choice: Table game center

Objective: During play times, Samisha will join her peers in play and maintain play with them for 10 minutes or more in cooperative play activities. She will show this in four different play areas.

What are you going to do? Point to or hand Samisha the game prop (e.g, car, ball).

What are you going to say? "Samisha, take a turn," or other appropriate prompt

How will you respond? If Samisha follows the instruction, praise and emphasize playing together. If not, hand Samisha the game prop and repeat instruction.

What materials do you need? Table games that can be used by two or more children at the same time (e.g., Don't Break the Ice, Lotto, Hungry Hungry Hippos)

How many opportunities will you provide each day?

Monday	Tuesday	Wednesday	Thursday	Friday
Free-choice: table games 10+ minutes	Free-choice: table games 10+ minutes	Free-choice: table games 10+ minutes	Free-choice: table games 10+ minutes	Free-choice: table games 10+ minutes

Figure 6.3. An ELO-at-a-Glance for Samisha. (*Source:* Horn, Lieber, Li, Sandall, & Schwartz, 2000.)

will have opportunities to play with a variety of puzzles, various building or manipulative toys, and materials that involve identifying or reproducing designs.

As a member of the child's IEP team, the consulting ECSE teacher can help write objectives that are functional and generative. An example would be "Annie will assemble toys or objects by putting pieces together. She will do this with at least five different toys available in the classroom, such as puzzles, LEGOs, or stringing beads." This new objective and the teaching procedures are stated on the ELO-at-a-Glance.

In preparing to use an ELO, the consulting ECSE teacher should work with the team to develop a learning objective or to modify the established learning objective so that it can be easily and naturally embedded in many activities (e.g., water play, cooking, art center) and routines (e.g., arrival, snack time, cleanup time). If a child needs instruction on a highly specific but necessary objective, however, using ELOs may not be the right approach. Here are some helpful hints for writing or tailoring learning objectives:

1. Do not limit a child's initiation of a skill or behavior to just one stimulus or cue. Instead of using a single cue, such as "When a toy is rattled or shaken, the child will crawl 4 feet to obtain the toy," try "Child will crawl a minimum of 4 feet in response to any of the following: adult presence, peer presence, to obtain objects, to participate in an activity, and so forth."
2. Broadly define the child's response, if appropriate. Instead of saying "Child will request help in obtaining a favorite toy that is out of reach," try "Child will solve common problems by using more than one strategy, such as using a tool, requesting help, reaching around the barrier, and so forth."
3. Avoid limiting the objective to one type of material. Instead of saying "Child will stack three 1-inch cubes," try saying, "Child will stack a variety of small, stackable items, including blocks, small books, notepads, plastic cups, LEGOs, and so forth."

The purpose is to translate an objective from a child's IFSP or IEP to a learning objective that can be addressed more easily and effectively in the classroom, home, or child care setting. The important features of tailoring the objective are that 1) teaching can be implemented within routine and planned activities, 2) teaching can be implemented across multiple activities so the child receives sufficient learning opportunities, and 3) teaching is aimed at the acquisition of new concepts and skills, not just practice of already acquired skills.

Organizing the Learning Objectives

Planning is key to effective use of ELOs. In essence, the teacher and team are using specially designed instruction and doing so within the ongoing activities and routines of the day. The team prepares for learning by selecting learning opportunities that are likely to occur and that are distributed throughout the day, and by preparing for learning by thinking carefully about the resources (including the people) that are available during class time. The team also prepares for learning by thinking about how they will monitor children's progress on their learning objectives.

Identifying or Creating Embedded Learning Opportunities A child's process of learning the objectives is supported by planned teacher behavior. Teachers create opportunities for a child to perform the behavior, and they act in such a way as to accelerate the child's acquisition of the behavior. One way to do this is to take advantage of a child's interests or preferences (one of the curriculum modifications) when planning for ELOs.

One of Nhan's objectives is to increase vocabulary. Nhan has learned to smile, select a toy or activity, and look busy as a way to avoid talking. However, his teachers also know that Nhan has some definite preferences in terms of toys. He likes to paint, build with blocks, and play ball on the playground. The teachers use the ELO strategy to teach Nhan to say the words for these toys. The teachers place the toys on shelves just out of his reach to encourage Nhan to ask for them by name. When he names the toy, a teacher gives it to him. Nhan's teacher also places pictures of all of the children's favorite toys and people, as well as small toys, in her pockets. During transition times, she pulls these out to play naming games with Nhan and his classmates.

Creating Multiple Embedded Learning Opportunities Multiple opportunities to practice targeted skills should be developed within and across activities. Children with special needs often need many opportunities to learn a new skill or concept. An important aspect of making ELOs work is to create many new opportunities to make certain that teaching and learning occur. Although existing activities are used during ELOs, the planning and instruction associated with this strategy is individualized and intentional. Use an activity matrix (see Chapter 4) to organize the learning opportunities.

Designing and Implementing Instruction

Selecting the appropriate teaching strategy can be difficult, but it is *so* important. The effective use of ELOs depends on designing and using instructional strategies that have a good chance of being effective. Fortunately, research and experience provide information to help make it easier to select good strategies (e.g., DEC, 2014; Sandall et al., 2005). Some of the things to think about in making selections include the following:

- Is the teaching strategy likely to be effective?
- Is it normalized? (Is it similar to the approaches used with all children, or will it stigmatize the child?)
- Is it useful across environments?
- Is it respectful of the child?

When planning and delivering ELOs, it is important to remember that there are three parts to a teaching episode—what the teacher says or does, what the child does, and how the teacher responds. The teacher or other adult must remember to complete the teaching episode by responding to the child. This is also called a *consequence*. It is planned ahead of time and might come in the form of praise, a comment, or a natural consequence, such as giving the child the toy he or she asked for. See Chapter 7 for more about instructional strategies.

Monitoring the Child's Progress Collecting data about the use of ELOs has two components. First, it is important to keep track of the opportunities that are actually provided. It can be difficult to do this in a busy and action-packed classroom. On the ELO-at-a-Glance, the teacher can make a hash mark each time an opportunity is provided. Some teachers attach a blank piece of paper to the wall and make tally marks there. In one classroom, the teacher decided to provide at least 10 opportunities for a particular child each day. He put 10 paper clips in his pocket. Each time he provided a learning opportunity for the child, he moved a paper clip to his other pocket.

Second, teachers, of course, want to know if a child is making progress. Is the child learning the skill or concept? Every week or two, the teacher (or the consulting ECSE teacher) should collect child performance data. If the child is making progress, the instruction should continue. If the child has achieved the objective, practice opportunities may continue, but the team should think about what objective to teach next. If the child is not making progress, the team should make a change. Thus, the team will have information that is directly related to the child's IFSP or IEP. Chapter 4 describes several ways to gather information about a child's progress: counts, notes, and permanent products. (See Chapter 4 for a more thorough discussion of these methods.) The data collection method chosen should match the objective, and it should be easy to implement in the classroom. The information is helpful only if it is collected and used regularly and systematically.

SUMMARY

ELOs have great natural appeal to teachers. This teaching strategy uses the existing activities, materials, and routines of the preschool classroom, home, or child care setting. Thus, it should be easy to incorporate a child's preferences and interests. ELOs naturally lead to the practice of behaviors that are distributed across the various times and events of classrooms and other learning environments.

It is important to remember, however, that ELOs are a way of providing specially designed instruction. It is not just about planning activities. ELOs must be carefully planned and carried out frequently enough to result in learning. They must also be matched to a child's individual learning objectives. The essential features of ELOs are contained on the ELO-at-a-Glance: the target behavior, what the teacher will do and say, how the child is expected to respond, and how the teacher will respond. It is vital that the teacher complete the teaching episode or learning opportunity by implementing all of these parts. Children with special needs have difficulty taking advantage of naturally occurring learning opportunities. Thus, an ELO is a specialized strategy that is used to deliver the individualized, deliberate instruction that some children need. The aim is for a child to learn his or her target objectives and to use them in meaningful ways. Success is measured by the child's progress. If the child is not making progress, even more instructional support is warranted. The next chapter describes what the team can do if the child needs even more specialized assistance.

Chapter 7

Child-Focused Instructional Strategies

Sometimes, children with special needs require directed, explicit instruction in order to achieve their learning objectives and take advantage of the typical early childhood curriculum. In such situations, teachers must use instruction that is more systematic, more frequent, and even more carefully planned than that described in previous chapters. Child-focused instructional strategies (CFIS) are, for the most part, the same strategies that are used in embedded learning opportunities (ELOs). The difference is the level of intensity with which instruction is provided. To acquire necessary skills and concepts, some children may need more opportunities every day to practice the skill, more assistance from their teachers, instruction in a setting with fewer distractions, positive reinforcement in a more consistent manner, and consistent guidance when they make errors.

These instructional strategies are techniques and methods for delivering instruction that have been demonstrated to result in improved child outcomes. They help teachers transform opportunities for learning into successful learning interactions (for more information on CFIS, see Grisham-Brown & Hemmeter, 2017; Schwartz, Ashmun, McBride, Scott, & Sandall, 2017). This chapter describes when and how to use these instructional strategies for young children who need specially designed instructional situations, and it defines and describes the strategies.

WHEN TO USE CHILD-FOCUSED INSTRUCTIONAL STRATEGIES

Child-focused instructional strategies can be used whenever you want to teach specific skills or concepts. The strategies can be used in a number of different classroom situations and during interactions that are child- or teacher-initiated. CFIS are used when

Table 7.1. Instructional interactions using child-focused instructional strategies

Adult (antecedent)	Child (target behavior)	Adult (consequence)
"Samisha, walk to the snack table."	Samisha walks with her walker to the snack table.	"All right, Samisha. Have a seat right here." The adult gives Samisha a smile and a pat on the arm.
At the snack table, the teacher says, "Anyone wearing an orange shirt can clean up."	Drew looks at his shirt and says, "I'm orange" and gathers his snack dishes.	"Great job listening for directions, Drew."
As the teacher is reading a book during circle time, she stops, points to a picture of a baseball bat, and says, "What is a word that rhymes with *bat*?"	Three children call out in unison, "cat."	The teacher responds, "You are correct. *Cat* rhymes with *bat*. Does anyone have another idea?"
At small group, Nhan and his peers are playing with multicolored interlocking cubes. The teacher creates a pattern with her cubes of blue-green-blue-green. She shows it to Nhan and says, "Finish the pattern."	Nhan hands her a blue cube and then a green cube.	"Thanks, Nhan! You figured out how to help me make an ABABAB pattern."

a teacher or the team has identified a learning objective and has determined that for a particular child to learn the objective, he or she needs specially designed instructional situations (e.g., "Samisha will use her walker or furniture to walk or step from place to place in the classroom"; "Nhan will use the Picture Exchange Communication System to request preferred art materials"). That is, these strategies are used when a child may need more intensive attention than can be embedded in ongoing classroom activities.

When using these teaching strategies, teams should remember that all instruction takes place in the context of an interaction. Most often, CFIS occur in the context of an adult–child interaction, but peers can also be effective teachers. Either the child or the adult can begin the interaction, but the adult makes the decision to use this interaction as an instructional opportunity and uses the planned teaching strategy. When thinking about instruction occurring in the context of interactions, it is important to consider the sequence of turns that the people involved take; ideally, an instructional interaction includes an antecedent, target behavior, and consequence. See Table 7.1 for examples.

These examples are explicit because they are planned by the teacher to help the child achieve his or her learning objective. During CFIS, these same instructions are used regularly, and the teacher evaluates the child's behavior and uses it as the basis for changing the teacher's behaviors. The purpose is to facilitate the child's success in learning the objective.

THE BASIC STEPS

The first step is to decide whether to use specially designed instructional situations in addition to ELOs, or if embedding instruction into the ongoing classroom activities and routines will be sufficient for a child to learn the targeted learning objective. Following are some of the criteria that the teacher and the team need to consider:

- *The child is making very slow progress despite the teacher's or the team's use of ELOs or curriculum modifications.* In other words, the child's response to the current intervention is not meeting the team's expectations. In this case, the team will add

CFIS to a specially designed instructional situation to provide the child with more opportunities to practice the target skill with guidance.

- *The child must learn a skill or concept to take advantage of or gain access to the general early childhood curriculum.* In other words, the target skill is a keystone skill that will help the student access the ongoing classroom activities and curricular content. Examples of such skills or concepts that might need to be taught explicitly to a young child are establishing joint attention, imitating children or adults, playing with toys, and following simple directions.
- *The child must learn a school survival skill.* That is, the teacher or the team teaches skills that help the child be as independent as possible in the classroom. The primary examples are age-appropriate adaptive skills that would be best taught in a private setting, such as toileting or dressing. Other examples include the skills needed to follow the classroom routine.
- *The child's objective is unique.* Other children in the classroom are not learning this skill or concept. Samisha's objective to learn to use her walker is one example; learning to use an augmentative and alternative communication system is another.

Once the decision is made to use CFIS, the basic steps are similar to those outlined for ELOs:

1. Clarify the learning objective and determine the criteria.
2. Gather baseline information to determine the child's current level of performance.
3. Use an activity matrix to select activities or times of the day when the special instruction can be delivered.
4. Design the instructional interaction, and write it on a planning form.
5. Implement the instruction as planned. Ensure that instruction is implemented correctly and frequently enough to provide multiple opportunities across the day for the child to respond and practice the skill with teacher guidance.
6. Collect and review child performance data daily.

Notice that the final step has changed in intensity. That is, the teacher or the team needs to collect child performance data daily so that informed teaching decisions can be made as soon as necessary. Because teacher and child time are valuable resources, the teacher needs to use classroom time wisely. Data are collected using one of the methods described in Chapter 4: counts, notes, or permanent products. Counting is often the preferred method.

Another way in which the use of CFIS differs from that of ELOs or curriculum modifications is the time that is identified for the specially designed instructional situation. The teacher may use a few minutes before or during an ongoing classroom activity for CFIS. For example, the teacher may join a child's play during free choice or outdoor time to target a specific skill or behavior using CFIS. The aim is to increase the number of opportunities that the child has to respond to explicit instruction on the targeted learning objective. Many children with learning differences will require many opportunities to learn a new skill. The data collected by the teacher will answer the question about how many trials are necessary for the child to learn the new skill.

DEVELOPING CHILD-FOCUSED INSTRUCTIONAL STRATEGIES

Whether a teacher plans to provide instruction embedded within an ongoing activity or routine or as a specially designed part of the day, the basic instructional strategies are the same. The strategies can be divided into three categories: instructions, prompting strategies, and consequence (e.g., positive reinforcement, corrective feedback) strategies.

Instructions

The purpose of *instructions* is to tell a child what he or she is expected to do. In a classroom, teachers may give instructions to a single child or to groups of children. An important step in giving good instructions is to know what it is that you want the child to do. Instructions guide the child to a specific component of a task or an activity or to the materials that you want the child to pay attention to. In general, good instructions are

- Short
- Clear
- Focused on the observable behavior
- Positive (i.e., they tell the child to *do* something rather than to *stop doing* something)

Table 7.2 provides examples of instructions.

Prompting Strategies

A *prompt* is something a teacher does before the child responds in order to increase the probability that the child will respond correctly. Many kinds of prompting strategies are useful in early childhood classrooms, but all should 1) help teach skills, 2) be removed as soon as possible (so the child can do the skill independently), and 3) be combined with reinforcement. Prompts may be verbal, gestural, a model, physical, or pictorial. Notice the different levels of support provided by the different

Table 7.2. Examples of good and poor instructions

Good instructions	Poor instructions
"Point to the train."	"I see lots of pretty pictures. Do you see a picture of a train?" (*Note:* The probable outcome of this instruction is for the child to say "Yes," not point to the picture.)
"Nhan, come play baseball with us."	"Nhan, look, lots of kids are playing baseball. You like baseball, don't you? What would you like to do now?"
"Write your name on the sign-in sheet."	"Remember what we do every day when we come into the classroom? It is the first thing we do; we do it before we join morning meeting. Remember, you get to sign in with everyone else from the class. You need to write your name right here."
(To a child who is running around the room during free-choice time)	
"Drew, listen. Do you want to play at the sensory table or with the blocks?"	"Drew, stop running around and think about what you want to do. You need to make a choice."

kinds of prompts. Prompt hierarchies (most-to-least or least-to-most) can be used systematically to teach new skills.

Graduated Guidance Using *graduated guidance,* a teacher provides the least amount of assistance necessary to the child. Remove the help as soon as the child can do the skill on his or her own.

Samisha is learning to put on her backpack by herself. This involves positioning the pack, putting one arm through the strap, pulling it to her shoulder, and then putting the other arm through the strap and extending her arm so that the strap is on her shoulder. The teacher uses a physical, hand-over-hand prompt for the steps of putting on the backpack that Samisha cannot do on her own and verbal prompts for the steps that Samisha can do but sometimes forgets. As soon as Samisha learns to do a new step on her own, the teacher no longer prompts that step.

Time Delay Teachers can reduce and eventually eliminate the prompts they give a child by allowing the child a few seconds to do part of the behavior before giving a prompt. This prompting strategy, called *time delay,* can be very effective in teaching children to be more spontaneous in requesting and labeling toys, materials, or activities.

Nhan's teacher uses time delay as a way to teach Nhan to use words to request items. At the art table, the teacher holds the art materials, looks expectantly at Nhan, and waits about 5 seconds or until Nhan uses words to request something (e.g., "brush," "paper"). Then the teacher gives him what he has asked for. If he does not ask, the teacher reminds him to ask by saying, "Tell me what you want."

Time delay is also an effective prompting strategy for nonverbal responses.

If Samisha always waits for the teacher to start putting the backpack on her, the teacher could use time delay. The teacher stands near the children's cubbies and says, "Time to get your backpacks on." Then he or she waits about 3 seconds while looking expectantly at Samisha. If Samisha begins the task, the teacher smiles and helps as needed. If Samisha waits, the teacher could give a more direct instruction, such as "Samisha, put your backpack on," and wait another 3 seconds.

Backward Chaining For some objectives, it may make more sense for the teacher to provide prompts or assistance for the entire sequence of steps at first.

Tina's teachers, Dolores and Maggie, use backward chaining to help Tina learn to fasten her clothing. At first, Dolores or Maggie use hand-over-hand assistance to get the fasteners lined up and to apply some pressure. Next, they start to remove their assistance during the last step (e.g., snapping the snaps, finishing the zip). Then, they start to remove their assistance at the step of applying pressure. Finally, they will remove their help at lining up the fasteners, and Tina will be able to do the whole series of steps by herself. While she is learning this series of steps, Tina experiences success at the completion of the task of fastening.

Consequence Strategies

A *consequence* is a teacher behavior or an environmental event that occurs after a child behavior. For example, if a child asks for a glass of water and someone brings the water, the consequence for the behavior of asking is receiving water. The most commonly used and most effective consequence in early learning settings is positive reinforcement. Another consequence frequently used is corrective feedback. Both of these are discussed further in this section.

Research and experience provide evidence to support the use of reinforcement procedures to help children learn. *Reinforcers* are things (e.g., words, activities) that follow a behavior. Instructions are prompts that occur before the child's behavior; reinforcers are what teachers do immediately after the child's behavior or response. The focus here is on the use of positive reinforcement.

Positive Reinforcement Positive reinforcement is something that follows a specific response and increases the likelihood that the response will happen again. Reinforcement is used extensively in educational environments and can be very simple and natural. For example, after a child asks for a ball, the teacher gives him or her the toy and says something like, "Thanks for asking. Here's the ball." It may be more systematic and formal: After Tina gets her clothes fastened, the teacher says, "Wow, Tina, you snapped your snaps!" and puts a star on her chart. Positive reinforcement is usually a pleasant consequence; it has a high probability of increasing whatever behavior it follows.

An important feature of positive reinforcement is that what functions as a reinforcer is very specific to each child and varies over time. Although teacher praise, encouragement, and smiles may be powerful reinforcers for most young children, you cannot assume that these will be effective for all children, especially with children with more significant disabilities. The only way to determine whether something is a reinforcer is to examine the effect it has on a child's behavior. For instance, if a child is not learning a skill in instructional sessions with teacher praise being used as the intended reinforcer, one interpretation may be that a more powerful reinforcer (e.g., access to a preferred toy, such as a music toy) may be needed.

Differential Reinforcement of Other Behavior The idea behind differential reinforcement of other behavior (DRO) is to catch the child being good and to let him or her know it! This technique is used when you want to decrease a challenging behavior in the classroom by providing the child with positive reinforcement for behaviors that are incompatible with the challenging behavior. For example, if a child is very active and moves rapidly from one activity to another without really playing at any activity, you could use a DRO procedure to provide feedback to the child when he or she does stay at an activity and becomes engaged in play. Call attention to the child's appropriate behavior ("Drew, look at you and Blake making a spaceship with the blocks. It's really getting big!"), rather than to his or her inappropriate behavior ("Drew, stop running around the classroom and find something to do!").

Corrective Feedback Sometimes, children give incorrect responses or engage in behavior that is not appropriate for the setting. Corrective feedback lets a child know when a response or behavior is incorrect or unacceptable and shows the child

Table 7.3. Examples of corrective feedback

Context/setting	Child behavior	Corrective feedback
During free play, Tina is playing with dolls in the dramatic play area with two other children.	Tina grabs a doll from another child.	"Tina, Amanda was playing with that doll. If you want a turn, you need to ask."
During specialized instructional time, Drew is working on identifying colors. The teacher holds up a blue container of bubbles and asks, "What color?"	Drew says, "Green."	"It is blue. Say *blue*."
The children are cleaning up after snack.	On his way to the trash can, Nhan drops his empty cup on the floor.	"Nhan, you dropped your cup. Go back and pick it up, please."

a more appropriate alternative. Corrective feedback should *never* be punitive. It offers the child information only and should be delivered in a neutral tone of voice. See Table 7.3 for some examples of corrective feedback.

The important elements of corrective feedback are that it provides the child with information about his or her behavior and provides guidance on how to improve the behavior.

Peer-Mediated Strategies

Teachers cannot be everywhere at once, so in some inclusive preschools, a teacher may rely on peers to assist children with special needs in learning or practicing some skills. To incorporate peers into an individualized program for a child with special needs, several points are important to remember (Barton & Smith, 2015; Schwartz & McBride, 2014).

- *The peer needs to know how to do the skill.* For example, if the objective for the child with special needs is to follow the routine of going outside, the peers who are helping should be able to do each step of going outside by themselves.
- *The peers need to know what to do to help the child with special needs learn the skill.* The teacher must explain to the peers exactly what they should do to help. For example, the teacher goes over each step of the routine with the peers. Peers should provide help only when the child cannot do a part of the task. For example, the child with special needs may be able to find his or her cubby when the teacher says, "Time to line up and go outside," but may have difficulty putting on his or her jacket all the way. The peers need to know to *not* provide help in finding the child's cubby but to provide help with the jacket.
- *Different peers should be incorporated into the learning process.* The teacher should choose several peers to be helpers for the child with special needs. One peer who is asked to be a helper all the time may grow tired of it.
- *The peers need to know that the teacher values their work.* Teachers can show how much they value the peers' assistance in several ways. They can praise them, give them a hug or pat, or provide a more formal reward, such as getting to do a special activity. Such adult recognition is a critical part of most peer-mediated teaching approaches.

- *The peers should be taught not to treat the child with special needs as the "helpee."* The teacher should point out the things that the child with special needs can do independently (i.e., recognize the child's strengths). In fact, sometimes it is appropriate to ask a child with special needs to be the peer helper. Also, when peers are giving too much assistance or assisting with things the child already knows how to do, the teacher needs to step in and suggest that they wait to see whether the child can do the task by him- or herself.
- *Remember that some of the curriculum modifications also involve peers but may require less time teaching the peers.* Examples are the ways that teachers group children for some activities, the use of peer buddies, and other simple modifications.

The examples in this chapter should guide teachers and their teams in the use of more explicit instruction. The forms in Chapter 4 provide direction for planning. Teachers may want to use the Instruction-at-a-Glance form (see Figure 7.1, Instruction-at-a-Glance for Tina, and the blank form in Appendix A) to guide the instructional episodes.

This planning form will help teachers highlight the elements necessary to implement CFIS and help them collect daily data on the child's performance. Note that on the second page of the Instruction-at-a-Glance, the number of the trials or opportunities is given. The teacher circles the number if the child is correct and slashes the number if the child is incorrect and uses the data to make instructional decisions.

TIPS FOR USING CHILD-FOCUSED INSTRUCTIONAL STRATEGIES

You should consider a number of issues when using CFIS and implementing the strategies described in this chapter. Additional resources to consult for using CFIS are found in Appendix B.

Scheduling

It may seem overwhelming to try to identify times during a busy day when the teacher or other adult can concentrate on a single child and provide specialized instruction. However, it is likely that this child is already demanding adult attention. For example, this may be the child that the teacher always has to help, remind, or have by his or her side. Why not use the time more productively? Here are some ideas:

- *Identify and use times when the other children are independent and engaged in activities.* This might be in the middle of free-choice time, out on the playground, or at snack time.
- *Select times that are followed by a fun or preferred activity.* The specially designed instructional time is hard work for a child; make sure it is followed by something fun.
- *Avoid selecting times that are the child's favorite or times when the child is successful in the classroom.* No one wants to leave something he or she enjoys or is good at.
- *Even a few minutes of special time is worth it.* Be consistent and provide this time every day. You and the child may be more successful if you select multiple short opportunities (i.e., 5 minutes) to work together rather than try to find one extended 30-minute block of time.

Instruction-at-a-Glance

Date: 2/11

Child's name: Tina Teacher's name: Dolores

Objective: With contextual cues, Tina will independently and accurately tell events that occurred on the same day at least 30 minutes after the occurrence of the event.

1. Setting for instruction

   When? End of work time

   Where? Near large-group area

   How often? 5 trials; repeat at recall time

   Materials needed? Pictures or toys from centers; review work time with Tina

2. Instructional interaction

Antecedent	Child behavior	Consequence
Instruction "What did you do at work time?" Wait 3 seconds.	Contextually accurate 2- to 3- word phrase (e.g., "I paint hearts.")	Positive reinforcement If correct, affirm and expand on response.
Prompt Model, such as "I paint hearts."		Corrective feedback If incorrect or no response, model.

(continued)

Figure 7.1. Instruction-at-a-Glance for Tina.

Figure 7.1. *(continued)*

Instruction-at-a-Glance

(continued)

3. Monitoring progress:

Instructions: For the numbers 5–0 and ND ("No data") in the columns representing number of trials, circle or draw a line through each number, depending on response: ◯ = correct, ⁄ = incorrect.

Date

Current step	2/11													
Will tell events that occurred on the same day immediately after work time	⑤	5	5	5	5	5	5	5	5	5	5	5	5	5
	~~4~~	4	4	4	4	4	4	4	4	4	4	4	4	4
	~~3~~	3	3	3	3	3	3	3	3	3	3	3	3	3
	②	2	2	2	2	2	2	2	2	2	2	2	2	2
	~~1~~	1	1	1	1	1	1	1	1	1	1	1	1	1
	~~0~~	0	0	0	0	0	0	0	0	0	0	0	0	0
Criteria: 80%	ND	ND	ND	ND	ND	ND	ND	ND	ND	ND	ND	ND	ND	ND

4. Comments, questions, or issues to discuss with the team:

The activity matrix (see Chapter 4) is an indispensable tool for scheduling. The activity matrix helps the teacher and team see the whole schedule and the many planned activities. They can then identify the best available times to provide frequent opportunities using CFIS to address an individual child's high-priority learning objective(s) and to distribute these opportunities throughout the day.

Selecting Materials

Here are some things to keep in mind when selecting materials for helping the child learn his or her specific learning objective:

- Use materials that are similar to those the child uses in the classroom or community.
- Use materials that the child finds interesting.
- Use materials that are developmentally appropriate.
- Use materials that are appropriate to the learning objective.
- Vary the materials.

Motivation

Not many people are motivated to work on something that is difficult without some added incentive. Here are some ideas for making CFIS time more enjoyable for children:

- Identify potential motivators. These can be activities such as getting more playground time, listening to music, or rocking in a rocking chair, or tangible motivators such as a favorite toy or a sticker. There are also social motivators, such as a smile and a pat on the back. Give the child choices from a set of potential motivators. Keep track of those the child prefers.
- During the teaching time, use a motivator along with the positive feedback you give to the child.
- Make sure the child receives these motivators at a rate that keeps the child trying the activity or working at the skill. For example, if a child likes to make paper chains, give the child a slip of paper as a tangible reinforcer for every correct response. When the child gets 10 (or at the end of the session), let the child make the paper chain. If the child is interested in letters, give the child a magnetic letter every time he or she makes a correct response, and spend time at the end of the session spelling words together. Here the idea is that you take an activity that the child likes (is reinforcing) and give the child "pieces" of the activity to keep working.
- If the special time involves more than one child, make sure the activity is motivating for everyone.

Monitoring Progress

It is important to collect regular data on the child's performance so that the teacher or the team can decide whether to continue the instruction or to change it. It is unfair to the child to continue doing the same thing if the child is not learning. The consulting ECSE teacher should devise a way of collecting these data so that the

Table 7.4. Troubleshooting for child-focused instructional strategies

Challenge	Potential solutions
The child is not progressing at an adequate rate on IFSP/IEP objectives.	Increase the intensity of instruction by providing more opportunities for the child to practice the skill with adult guidance. Replace the reinforcer with something you think will be more motivating for the child. Break down the objective into smaller steps; teach each of these intermediate objectives.
The child demonstrates challenging behavior during instructional sessions.	Shorten the sessions. Provide more positive reinforcement. Alternate the new tasks the child is learning with skills the child already knows how to do; that is, alternate between acquisition tasks and maintenance or practice tasks.
The child becomes dependent on prompts and waits for the teacher's instructions or assistance before trying to complete the task independently.	Decrease the amount of physical guidance. Increase the amount of time between giving a direction and providing assistance.
The data collected indicate that the child performs inconsistently depending on which teacher is working with him.	Examine the fidelity with which the intervention is being implemented. Is everyone on the team following the procedure as written and presenting it the same way to the child?
Team members believe that they have "done everything," but the child is still not making progress.	Examine the targeted learning objective and how it was selected. Team members should ask themselves these questions: Did you use a curriculum to select the goal? Are you addressing the correct spot in the scope and sequence for this particular child at this time in his or her learning history? Do you need to back up and teach some keystone or entry skills?

Key: IFSP, individualized family service plan; IEP, individualized educational program.

ECE teacher or assistants can carry out the plan, given the time and resources available to them. The Instruction-at-a-Glance (Figure 7.1) provides space for regular data collection along with guidance for delivering instruction. It may be the consulting ECSE teacher's responsibility to do a check or mini-test every few days to make sure that the child is learning the skill or concept.

Troubleshooting

Although many children will start making progress quickly with intensive instruction, some will provide challenges for the teacher and the educational team. See Table 7.4 for some ideas for troubleshooting instructional plans for children who are not making progress at the rate the team expects.

SUMMARY

This chapter describes how and when teachers and teams use more explicit CFIS. The strategies themselves (i.e., using good instructions, prompting, and using appropriate consequences) are similar to the strategies used for ELOs. The primary difference is the intensity with which instruction is provided. Sometimes, children continue to have difficulty with learning despite rich and inviting activities and environments and despite teachers' attempts to provide additional learning opportunities. Some children have very individual learning needs that demand more explicit instruction. In any case, it is the team's responsibility to ensure that sufficient and appropriate teaching occurs.

SECTION III

Important Topics Related to the Building Blocks Framework

The first seven chapters of this book described practices that can be used in a variety of early childhood classrooms. The last four chapters demonstrate how to apply the Building Blocks framework in four important topic areas. Why discuss these specific topics? According to the child development literature, many important developmental tasks are accomplished during the early childhood years. Furthermore, certain content areas and skills are becoming increasingly vital to ECE teachers and families. These topic areas are highlighted in outcome frameworks and overall program goals that have been established by the Office of Head Start in the Early Learning Outcomes Framework (see https://eclkc.ohs.acf.hhs.gov/sites/default/files/pdf/elof-ohs-framework.pdf), the U.S. Department of Education, OSEP's Child Outcomes (see http://ectacenter.org/outcomes.asp), as well as individual states' early learning standards and guidelines (see https://childcareta.acf.hhs.gov/sites/default/files/public/state_elgs_web_final_2.pdf). We identified these four topics and show how the Building Blocks framework can be applied:

- Independent behavior
- Acquiring and using knowledge
- Friendships and social relationships
- Developmentally appropriate classroom behavior

These areas differ from traditional areas of academic achievement and are linked to successful outcomes for all young children—a reminder that children with disabilities are children first. These areas, however, may be particularly problematic for children with disabilities and other special needs, requiring teachers in inclusive classrooms to pay special attention to how they address the areas.

Chapter 8

Becoming More Independent

Tina attends Head Start at the community center in her neighborhood. Her teachers and her mother are pleased with her progress. She participates in the classroom activities and plays with the other children in the classroom. She has learned many new skills and concepts this year. As part of her kindergarten transition plan, the consulting ECSE teacher, Tamika, observed Tina in her classroom. Tamika was concerned by Tina's lack of independence in the classroom. She observed that a teacher or another child was always available to help Tina make transitions, complete tasks, and manage her materials. Tamika wondered what the team could do to help Tina learn some independence skills (e.g., hang up her backpack in her cubby, clean up after a task) that will help her succeed in kindergarten.

Independence includes being able to rely on oneself and one's own ability, being self-confident, and being self-reliant. These valued characteristics appear to be related to school and work success. They have also been identified by OSEP and the Office of Head Start as important outcomes for young children who participate in federally funded early learning programs. Independent behavior in general is related to how children take care of themselves, accomplish their basic needs, and interact with the world around them. Although it is premature to talk about children's taking care of themselves, living on their own, or making vocational choices when they are in preschool, some of the foundational skills and behaviors taught in preschool serve children throughout their lifetimes. Independence skills are foremost among these important and functional skills. Independent classroom behavior in preschool includes but is not limited to

- Making independent transitions within the classroom and school (e.g., walking from the classroom to the playground without holding the teacher's hand)
- Managing personal possessions and classroom materials appropriately (e.g., hanging up coat and backpack in cubby)
- Completing developmentally appropriate tasks without adult assistance
- Staying engaged in an appropriate play activity
- Actively participating in a developmentally appropriate group activity
- Appropriately completing self-care tasks, such as those involved in toileting, dressing, eating, and personal hygiene (e.g., nose care)

The ability to stick to a task and complete it independently is highly valued by kindergarten and elementary school teachers, yet these skills are often not explicitly taught in preschool classrooms. In fact, children's opportunities to be independent or to practice doing things by themselves are often preempted. This chapter suggests strategies that can be used in inclusive early childhood classrooms to help children develop and practice appropriate independent behavior. (For further reading about helping children become more independent, see Azrin & Foxx, 1989; Baker & Brightman, 2004; Schwartz et. al., 2017.)

EXECUTIVE FUNCTION

Executive function plays an important role in helping children learn a number of valued skills, including independence skills (Diamond & Lee, 2011; McClelland, & Cameron, 2018). Executive function includes those skills that "make it possible to sustain attention, keep goals and information in mind, refrain from responding immediately, resist distraction, tolerate frustration, consider the consequences of different behaviors, reflect on past experiences, and plan for the future" (Zelazo, Blair, & Willoughby, 2016, p. 1). Three specific skills that fall under the umbrella term of *executive function* are cognitive flexibility, working memory, and inhibitory control. Young children, especially those with special needs, may need specially designed instruction to acquire these important skills. Teachers can assist children in acquiring the skills associated with executive function by

- Ensuring that children have opportunities to engage in physical activity every day
- Incorporating music, dance, and activity in the classroom
- Supporting pretend play in which children take on different roles
- Scaffolding new learning with visual supports
- Teaching children to take turns
- Helping children learn to label and recognize their feelings

- Assisting children to persist with challenging and multistep activities
- Systematically increasing demands so that children can practice executive function skills

As with other skills and behavior, teachers can use the Building Blocks framework to help children acquire executive function skills. Teachers identify the key behavior(s) and provide the appropriate support that the child needs to acquire and practice executive function skills. Simple modifications may provide the conditions for the child to demonstrate developing skills. Teachers can embed opportunities for instruction on executive function into ongoing classroom activities and routines, including play and games.

For example, in order to help Tina be more independent during classroom transitions, her teachers have decided to select focused attention, a subskill of executive function. This skill requires Tina to learn to pay attention to the current task and activity. Tina's teachers are going to begin teaching Tina this skill by modifying the curriculum with visual supports. At every transition, a teacher will give Tina a picture or symbol specifying the expectations of the transition (e.g., a picture of the table when it is time to go to small groups). The teacher gives Tina the picture accompanied by a very clear direction. When Tina makes the transition successfully, the teacher provides behavior-specific praise, commenting on how Tina is in the desired location alongside her friends. As Tina becomes more successful during transitions, the teachers decrease the individualized support that they are providing.

TEACHING INDEPENDENCE SKILLS

One of the first steps in teaching children to be more independent is to determine which skills to target. It is very important to remember that children cannot and should not be expected to complete a skill or behavior independently until they can complete it accurately and fluently under adult supervision. Once children have shown mastery of skills, it is time to help them become more independent with those skills. Therefore, independent performance can be thought of as another level of skill acquisition; teachers must begin to plan for independence in the same way they plan for generalization and maintenance. Although it may not be necessary for children to demonstrate some skills independently in preschool, it is important for teachers and parents to consider the expectations that children will encounter in their next school setting, especially in the few months before children make the transition to that setting.

Next, team members need to determine when and how they are going to teach independence. Like any new skill, independence must be taught. This includes providing multiple opportunities across the day to be independent and systematically decreasing the amount of support the child receives while maintaining appropriate child behavior. The steps outlined in Chapter 4 may help a teacher or the team to identify the child's learning needs and plan how to teach the identified skills.

Once the team has decided which skill to target for independence, the team needs to assess how much support the child is currently receiving to complete the task. When teaching independence, select tasks that have steps the child can complete independently. For example, if a teacher wants to teach the child to hang up his or her coat and backpack on arrival in the classroom, the teacher needs to be sure that the child can currently complete all the steps of that task with adult supervision. Then, the teacher needs to determine how much teacher and peer support is currently provided to complete the task. For example, can the child do it if a teacher is standing right next to him or her? Does the teacher need to talk the child through the task and provide constant encouragement to keep going?

When describing the amount of support or prompting a child currently receives, consider three categories of prompting: physical support, instructional support, and environmental support. Physical support includes proximity, any touching of the child (e.g., holding his or her hand during transitions), and physically helping a child complete a step of the task (e.g., turning on the water during hand washing). Instructional support includes teacher directions, comments, praise, and encouragement. Environmental support includes any type of pictures, process charts, or other visual supports that the teacher has displayed to facilitate child performance (e.g., steps to washing hands posted over the sink). Understanding the amount of support a child currently receives helps teachers determine which tasks are good candidates for independence training and how to change their own behaviors to facilitate a child's independence.

The next step is to determine when to teach the identified skills. Using the activity matrix, the team can plan times of the day when all of the children will work on independent tasks or schedule times to provide specially designed instruction on target skills for individual children. For some teachers, one of the most difficult parts of teaching independence skills is providing children with opportunities to be independent. It is easy to fall into the habit of offering help rather than giving children a little extra time and opportunity to complete the task independently. To avoid this, teachers can schedule their own activities on the activity matrix. If a child can already put his or her things in the cubby but always waits for help, then the teacher can welcome the child at the first activity of the day rather than while standing at the cubbies. If the child needs instruction in the steps involved in becoming independent, the teacher can schedule him- or herself to be nearby.

The next step is to begin the independence training. When planning the intervention, teams should consider what they expect the child to do and what the adults will do while the child is working independently. Do any special materials need to be prepared or organized in a particular way to facilitate child independence? Remember that as the amount of support provided for the child decreases, praise and encouragement are still necessary. In planning this part of the intervention, it may be helpful to spend a day observing a classroom that represents the child's next school environment or next age group (e.g., kindergarten) to see the level of independence demonstrated by the children in that classroom. It is most helpful to observe early in the year to get an idea of what children are doing at the beginning of the school year.

It is also important to remember that cultural traditions and beliefs about children influence notions about developmentally appropriate independence. For example, the norms for independent eating vary from one culture to another. Teachers and their team members should learn about the beliefs of families in their programs and reflect on their own beliefs regarding independence.

Finally, to teach children independence, teachers need to provide children with multiple opportunities to practice independence throughout the day and across different activities. Begin with small steps. If children are learning to walk in the halls without holding the teacher's hand, it does not mean that the teacher can never hold children's hands; it simply means that the teacher does not *need* to hold their hands. Children can also learn to complete work independently early in preschool. When children are working on tabletop activities (e.g., puzzles, manipulatives, visual discrimination tasks such as matching parquetry blocks), they should be encouraged to complete the activity independently. Often, in an attempt to be helpful, adults preempt children's opportunities to develop the ability to do things by themselves. Children, however, need these opportunities to develop self-reliance and self-confidence, so perhaps the most important part of teaching independent classroom behavior is to provide opportunities for children to be independent and to support their accomplishments.

Tina's teachers asked the consulting ECSE teacher to help them pinpoint Tina's learning needs in the area of independence. Together they decided to begin working on greater independence at the learning centers using embedded learning opportunities (ELOs). Their observations told them that although Tina's picture schedule helped her improve her executive function skills and move from activity to activity, she was often slow to begin the transition. Consequently, a peer was often asked to hold her hand to help her get to the next activity. The teachers planned a new intervention that they used for all the children. Everyone was told to make the transition "all by yourself," and a highly preferred event followed for those who got to the next activity by themselves. Tina received a selected reinforcer if she was one of the first to make the transition. After a week, the new plan appeared to be working.

Table 8.1 provides additional examples of instructional support at each level of the Building Blocks framework. Use the information presented in the table to spark your own ideas about providing the level of support a child needs.

SUMMARY

Independence does not appear as a separate domain in most early childhood curricula, yet independent behavior is valued and implicit in many aspects of a curriculum. For children, *independence* refers to managing one's personal needs and adapting one's behaviors to the social expectations of the teachers and the other children in the group. Learning these kinds of skills is often a factor in a child's successful participation in community-based classrooms and other activities.

Executive function skills develop over the early childhood years and into adolescence. These skills may be found in the Approaches to Learning domain or across several of the traditional curricular domains. Teachers facilitate these skills through provision of high-quality early education programs and scaffolded opportunities to develop and practice executive function skills and self-regulation.

All young children are provided with learning opportunities to be more independent. For example, their teachers help them learn to put on their shoes and coats,

Table 8.1. Examples of instructional strategies supporting independent classroom behavior using the Building Blocks framework

Building Block	Strategies
Child-focused instructional strategies (CFIS)	Teach children the play skills needed to participate in classroom activities.
	Teach children the self-help skills needed to perform and participate in routine events; gradually decrease the adult's support to encourage independence.
	Teach children the steps involved in completing classroom routines, such as putting materials in their cubby, getting ready to go outside or come back inside, getting ready for snack time, or cleaning up after playtime; gradually decrease the adult's support to encourage independence.
	Use behavior-specific praise and tangible reinforcers as necessary to teach children to persist with difficult and multistep activities
Embedded learning opportunities (ELOs)	Provide opportunities for children to practice the steps in classroom routines.
	Incorporate independence skills within relevant classroom themes or projects (e.g., practice brushing teeth to a special song, do a project on shoes to offer practice putting on shoes).
	Add a "finished box" to appropriate activities (e.g., when children are finished writing in their journal, they can put the journal in the "finished box").
	Use visual supports to teach children to take on different roles during pretend play.
Curriculum modifications (CMs)	Use process charts for hand washing and other tasks to help children remember all the steps.
	Place materials at children's level so that they can get them by themselves.
	Allow extra time for children to complete a task without adult assistance.
	Use pictures or objects to help children remember where they are going during a transition.
	Use pictures, labels, or special containers to help children be more independent during cleanup time.
	Use preferred materials and rotate materials in the learning centers to encourage engagement.
High-quality early childhood environment	Have developmentally and chronologically age-appropriate expectations for all children.
	Provide opportunities for children to experiment with new tasks, materials, and activities.
	Include opportunities for children to do things independently, and have adults available when children request assistance.
	Provide a predictable schedule, routines, and staff.
	Provide facilities and equipment that are the appropriate size for young children.
	Provide opportunities for group physical activities, such as dance or yoga.

follow classroom routines, and persist in solving problems. Children with disabilities or other special needs may need modifications to the materials or the skills, extra practice, or more deliberate teaching in order to learn independence, however. This chapter reminds teachers to evaluate their own behaviors so that they do not provide too much help. The Building Blocks framework can guide teachers in offering the right amount of help.

Chapter 9

Acquiring and Using Knowledge: Literacy and STEAM

Samisha's teacher helps her off the bus. Samisha holds two bear-shaped pieces of brown construction paper. She is excited to tell her teacher that she read two books from the classroom literacy bag last night. The teacher notices that Samisha's grandmother has written the title of each book on the bears, and Samisha has written her name on them. Samisha gives the literacy bag containing the two books back to her teacher.

Later that day, Samisha is playing at the dramatic play area, which is decorated as a doctor's office. Two of Samisha's classmates are sitting in child-size chairs and looking through magazines while they wait to see the "doctor." Samisha is examining the classroom aide. Samisha holds a clipboard with a piece of paper that has pictures and words for different body parts. The aide prompts Samisha to attend to the pictures and words as she conducts the checkup. Soon, the teacher rings the bell, and after cleaning up, the children rush over to story time. These activities are all part of the teachers' plan to support the early literacy skills of Samisha and her classmates.

Mateo's teacher, Dara, and the morning assistant, Aisha, are watching the children in the backyard. Dara suggests that they organize a walk around the yard, so they bundle Mateo and some of the younger children into wagons, assign older children as "wagon-pullers," give each child a bag, and set off on a walk along the fence. Dara encourages children to look for leaves, sticks, and flowers and lets children pick them up and collect them in their bags. Later, they empty their bags onto the sensory table.

IMPORTANCE OF ACQUIRING AND USING KNOWLEDGE

The early childhood years are a time of remarkable development and learning. Young children learn a great deal about language and literacy, mathematics, science, and the arts before they enter kindergarten. Much research has focused on early language and literacy knowledge and skills (e.g., Hart & Risley, 1995; Schatschneider, Fletcher, Francis, Carlson, & Foorman, 2004) and recognizes the importance of a strong start in early literacy for later academic success. Research on early language and literacy has influenced the learning experiences provided in early childhood programs. More recently, science, technology, engineering, art, and math (STEAM) have garnered increased attention. For example, early math knowledge is one of the strongest predictors of successful math grades in high school, high school graduation, and even college entry (Fuson, Clements, & Sarama, 2015). Furthermore, STEAM curriculum helps children focus, learn new vocabulary, collaborate with one another, and develop scientific relationships (Moomaw & Davis, 2010). Early childhood programs with integrated creative arts are linked with greater emotional regulation (Brown & Sax, 2013), social skills (Lobo & Winsler, 2006; Ritblatt, Longstreth, Hokoda, Cannon, & Weston, 2013), and receptive language abilities (Brown, Benedett, & Armistead, 2010).

Acquiring and using concepts and skills in all of these areas are important outcomes for all young children, including those with special needs. The OSEP of the U.S. Department of Education identified "acquiring and using knowledge and skills" as an essential child outcome (http://ectacenter.org/outcomes.asp). This broad outcome includes the precursor skills that enable children to be successful in the academic content of formal schooling, and it also recognizes that children learn and use these skills when they play, explore, and interact with the people and things in their environments. The Head Start Early Learning Outcomes Framework (U.S. DHHS, 2015) includes the domains of language, literacy, and cognition—including mathematics and scientific reasoning—in their description of what all young children should know and be able to do. Similarly, state early learning standards and guidelines include many of these domains.

High-quality early childhood classrooms provide young children with many opportunities for early literacy learning, such as listening to storybook read-alouds, singing, looking at self-selected books, drawing and writing, acting out stories, and exploring reading and writing materials. Likewise, high-quality early childhood classrooms promote STEAM learning by providing children with opportunities to explore and investigate, ask questions, gather information, and solve problems, as well as by furnishing materials that encourage active observation and exploration. Although literacy experiences are common in early childhood programs, math and other STEAM topics may appear far less frequently. Observational studies have found very little or no time spent in math learning experiences (e.g., Farran, Lipsey, Watson, & Hurley, 2007). Such findings underscore the need for intentional planning and teaching.

WHAT ARE THE COMPONENTS OF EARLY LITERACY AND STEAM

A research-based, comprehensive core curriculum provides the foundation for the early childhood classroom. In addition, domain-specific (i.e., mathematics, science, early literacy) research-based curricula are also available. See the Early Childhood

Table 9.1. Literacy concepts

Literacy concept	Description
Oral language, vocabulary, and concepts	Children expand and use their vocabularies and concept knowledge.
Concepts about print	Children gain understanding of print concepts, such as English text is written left to right and top to bottom.
Print functions	Children understand the various functions of print in signs, books, and so forth.
Alphabet knowledge	Children gain ability to recognize and name the letters of the alphabet.
Phonemic awareness	Children gain ability to recognize and manipulate the sounds in spoken language.
Knowledge of text structures	Children gain understanding that text has different structures such as the beginning, middle, and end of a story.
Writing	Children have frequent opportunities for emergent writing every day.
Storybook reading	Children have frequent opportunities to listen to books every day.

Learning and Knowledge Center for reviews of early childhood curricula (https://eclkc.ohs.acf.hhs.gov/curriculum/article/choosing-preschool-curriculum). The key components of the early literacy curriculum are found in Table 9.1. The key components of the STEAM curriculum are found in Table 9.2.

PROMOTING LITERACY AND STEAM

To develop and learn the many concepts and skills referenced in Tables 9.1 and 9.2, children need many opportunities. Furthermore, they need to take advantage

Table 9.2. STEAM curricular concepts

STEAM curricular concept	Description
Earth, physical, and life sciences	Observation, prediction, and using evidence to support answers. Children can also learn about scientific content, such as weather, energy, ecosystems, plants, animals, motion, stability, and life cycles.
Technology	Children explore technology by observing and using simple tools and machines.
Engineering	Children can explore early engineering skills through building models, trying out new ideas, and designing structures.
Number concepts and quantities	Children understand that numbers represent quantities and have ordinal properties (e.g., number words represent a rank order, particular size, position in a list).
Number relationships and operations	Children understand and use numbers to describe relationships and solve problems.
Geometry and spatial sense	Children understand shapes and their properties and how objects are related to one another.
Patterns	Children recognize patterns, sequencing, and critical thinking skills necessary to predict and classify objects in a pattern.
Measurement and comparison	Children understand attributes and relative properties of objects as related to size, capacity, and area.
Creative arts	Children express creativity and imagination through thinking, play, imagination, and interactions with others; they use various media.

Key: STEAM, science, technology, engineering, arts, and math.

of these opportunities and actively participate in them. Teachers promote their learning by selecting and implementing a research-based curriculum and by creating a literacy-rich and STEAM-rich learning environment. The universal design for learning (UDL) principles can be used to help teachers use their curriculum and design their environments for the wide diversity of learners in their classrooms. Teachers think about how to provide a variety of ways to gain access to and acquire new knowledge and skills and to demonstrate what children are learning. Teachers do this by ensuring multiple means of representation (e.g., words, symbols), multiple means of expression (e.g., talking, moving, drawing), and multiple means of engagement (e.g., trying over and over, watching and doing).

In planning for this solid foundation for literacy and STEAM learning, teachers consider at least three aspects of their learning environment: 1) designing interest areas, 2) selecting and displaying toys and materials, and 3) integrating literacy and STEAM across the activities and routines.

Designing Interest Areas

Well-designed interest areas or free-choice centers are organized; they attract and maintain children's attention, and they provide options for participation and expression. *Literacy centers* are specific learning environments designed to facilitate the development of early literacy knowledge and skills, and at least two such centers are important—a library or book center and a writing center. To facilitate the development of STEAM knowledge and skills, teachers consider how they use their sensory table and rotate the sensory items. They make their science center a place that attracts children's attention and offers tools and resources for investigations, enliven their construction center to include opportunities for building and tinkering, and even make a "creation station" with all sorts of materials for arts and crafts.

Selecting and Displaying Toys and Materials

Toys and materials represent children's interests as well as the curricular goals. Materials should grab and keep children's attention, provoke curiosity and imagination, and allow children to explore and extend their learning. Both open-ended materials, such as playdough, sticks, and sand, and close-ended materials, such as puzzles and stacking toys, have a place in the classroom. Unexpected materials such as mechanical toys, pulleys, and magnifying glasses encourage reasoning and problem solving. Use materials that represent cultural and linguistic as well as ability diversity.

Integrating Literacy and STEAM

Planning for literacy is more than selecting and reading a storybook at circle time. Likewise, STEAM is more than counting and setting up a science center. All of these skills can be integrated across daily activities and routines. In fact, distributing this content across the day will increase children's learning opportunities and likely make those opportunities more interesting. Mathematizing is an example.

Mathematizing is about bringing out the math in what children are doing. Teachers talk about and ask questions related to the math concepts and skills in everyday activities. They count out loud as they pass out snacks and comment that they will need the same number of spoons. They look for shapes when out on the playground and encourage children to find the shapes.

USING THE BUILDING BLOCKS FRAMEWORK

Some children may not take full advantage of the environment and materials and some may have difficulty participating in the planned lessons and activities. Through their careful observation and assessment, the teacher and team will notice the child who is struggling or not making expected progress. The Building Blocks framework and the planning procedures described in previous chapters can help teachers provide individual children with the level of support or assistance needed.

One of the first steps is to determine which skills or which subskills to teach. A curriculum checklist may help to pinpoint the difficulty. Next, determine when and how to teach the skill. This means determining the level of support the child needs. A simple modification may be enough or the child may need more specially designed instruction. The team also decides when to provide learning opportunities throughout the day. They create their teaching plans and use the activity matrix to make sure that many intentionally planned opportunities occur. They also clarify their plans for collecting data and monitoring the child's performance. They use this information to update and adjust their teaching plans.

Samisha's team is pleased with the literacy instruction in their classroom, but as they looked at the kindergarten assessment the children would soon take, they worried that they had not spent enough time on math and other curriculum areas. They used a math checklist to find out what the children had learned about early math concepts and skills. They noticed lots of variability in children's ability to count, identify shapes, add (put together) and subtract (take away), and measure. They then plan a unit on measurement. They also increase learning opportunities by mathematizing books during story time. They select several books that lend themselves to mathematizing: *The Very Hungry Caterpillar* (Carle, 1969), *Go Dog Go!* (Eastman, 1961), and *Last Stop on Market Street* (de la Peña, 2015). They use questioning strategies (Hintz & Smith, 2013) to encourage math thinking. The teachers also notice that Samisha is not yet associating numerals with quantities, so they select and make new games for the games table and plan to embed instruction for Samisha on this skill during free-choice time.

Aisha is excited to tell Dara what she's been learning about science in the early childhood curriculum course she is taking at college. She describes some of the videos she has seen and brings copies of handouts about science for young children. She tells Dara that the walks they take with the children are great science activities. Together, Dara and Aisha look at the state early learning standards, find science standards for even the youngest children, and check to see the

Table 9.3. Examples of strategies for facilitating early literacy skills using the Building Blocks framework

Building Block	Strategies
Child-focused instructional strategies (CFIS)	Use prompting and reinforcement techniques to systematically teach a child to look at a book.
	Use direct instruction and graduated guidance to teach a child who is making the transition to kindergarten to write his or her name.
	Use time delay to increase commenting when a child is looking at a preferred book.
	Use visual support strategies and systematically fade those prompts to teach a child to answer questions about a story.
Embedded learning opportunities (ELOs)	Address holding a writing utensil through a preferred activity, such as signing up to use the computer.
	Address language comprehension (an important prerequisite to reading comprehension) by reading stories and asking questions about preferred topics.
	Target letter sounds by using alphabet blocks in the construction area.
	Use Scrabble or other spelling game to enhance matching skills and patterning skills with letter tiles.
Curriculum modifications (CMs)	Use books about highly preferred topics.
	Use modified writing materials (e.g., foam grips on pens).
	Use modified writing surfaces (e.g., slant boards, tabletop easels).
	Increase name recognition by requiring children to sign up for highly preferred centers and jobs using name tags.
High-quality early childhood environment	Construct literacy-rich centers, including but not limited to a library center, a writing center, and literacy and writing props in the dramatic play center.
	Create a print-rich classroom.
	Schedule regular story times.
	Conduct phonological awareness activities, including rhyming and sound awareness.

expectations for the children in their child care home. They see that Mateo should be showing lots of interest in natural elements, and he should also be experimenting by dumping and filling containers. They realize that they are already providing opportunities, but they also realize that Mateo isn't always interested in the activities. Dara and Aisha write short lesson plans for Mateo and create a new activity matrix that reminds them when to provide extra support for his learning.

For more ideas for applying the Building Blocks framework to early literacy and STEAM, see Tables 9.3 and 9.4.

SUMMARY

This chapter describes early literacy and STEAM and their importance in early childhood classrooms. These curricular areas involve many concepts and skills. Learning in these areas is complex, but it can also be fun. The selected

Table 9.4. Examples of strategies for facilitating early STEAM skills using the Building Blocks framework

Building Block	Strategies
Child-focused instructional strategies (CFIS)	Use prompting and reinforcement techniques to systematically teach a child to match shapes.
	For the child who has difficulty following directions, make and use picture cards to teach how to follow sequential steps; use the cards for activities such as science experiments.
	Locate software that virtually manipulates objects and numerals for the child with limited hand strength to touch and count, add, and subtract.
	Use time delay to encourage a child to offer solutions to simple problems that you create and practice during a quiet time.
Embedded learning opportunities (ELOs)	Insert prediction questions such as "what will happen next . . ." or "I wonder what will happen" at planned times during the day, to practice reasoning and prediction.
	During transition times, have children identify numerals, have the target child practice "his/her" numerals.
	Make comparisons with plates at snack time, shoes in the dramatic play area, and rocks in the science center.
	Select the science vocabulary for the week; teach the words to the child at small-group time before using at the whole-group activity.
	Make time for the child to build simple machines or structures at small-group time in addition to opportunities in the block area or construction center.
Curriculum modifications (CMs)	Provide lots of loose materials such as cardboard tubes, paper, cotton balls, string, small containers, and so forth; give each child a cardboard box and let the child select his or her building supplies.
	Give the child a symbol or picture card to remind the child of his or her step in the group cooking project.
	Create a weather station at one of the free-choice centers; let children make individual weather charts.
	Provide collections of preferred natural materials (e.g., pine cones, shells), and encourage counting.
	Use a touch screen or other adaptation for a child to participate in learning games or activities.
High-quality early childhood environment	Have children select their part of the science experiment; some manipulate materials, some write/draw observations, some make predictions.
	During music activities, give children choices of musical instruments or dancing to the music.
	Include nonfiction books on STEAM-related topics.
	Add artifacts or photos from nature walks and field trips to the science center.
	Have children use a variety of creative means (e.g., dance, movement, visual arts) to express their ideas and interests.

Key: STEAM, science, technology, engineering, arts, and math.

research-based curricula will provide information on the sequence for learning, and the curricula may also provide lessons for whole-group or small-group activities. These lessons provide guidance for promoting play, exploration, and conversations that contribute to children's learning of literacy and STEAM skills. For children who need additional support, the Building Blocks framework can be applied to individualize their learning.

Chapter 10

Friendships and Social Relationships

Although Nhan is interested in his peers, he is not very successful at initiating interactions with them. The other children do not seem to mind having him around, but they do not seek him out, and he does not show any peer preferences. Nhan's teachers are concerned that he is spending more and more time in solitary play activities, and they are not sure what to do.

Mr. Alvarez is a first-year teacher in an inclusive ECE program. During his master's degree program, he was always very interested in the classes about social development. He had planned to implement innovative social interaction strategies in his classroom, but so far he is overwhelmed with the day-to-day logistics of running the classroom. What can he do to implement these strategies?

Developing positive peer relationships is a major developmental accomplishment of early childhood. In the context of peer relationships, children develop important communication, social, play, and cognitive skills, as well as gain emotional support. Playful social interactions with peers are an essential part of the early childhood years and "positive social-emotional skills (including social relationships)" have been identified as one of the child outcomes for young children with special needs by OSEP of the U.S. Department of Education (Early Childhood Technical Assistance Center, p. 1). The Head Start Early Learning Outcome Framework (U.S. DHHS, 2015) also identifies social and emotional learning, and specifically developing relationships with peers, as an important outcome for toddlers and preschoolers.

The development of positive social skills and social relationships is predictive of school, work, and leisure outcomes (Goldstein, Lackey, & Schneider, 2014).

Three main concepts to consider regarding young children's social relationships include *friendships, social acceptance,* and *social rejection.* These terms are not discrete but rather points along a continuum of relationships that occur in an inclusive classroom. Two children are *friends* when they choose to play with each other more than with other children. More than acquaintances, these children often seek to sit beside each other in class or to walk with each other during transitions. True friendships are reciprocal—both children identify each other as friends and are equally likely to initiate interactions—and are characterized by mutual enjoyment and positive affect (Buysse, Goldman, West, & Hollingsworth, 2008). *Social acceptance* means that other children in the class play with the child; they smile at the child and are happy to sit beside him or her at snack time. Whereas friendship is an active relationship, social acceptance is more passive. Some children in preschool classrooms are *socially rejected.* Peers in the class may not choose the child to play with, they may ask the child to leave a play activity or will leave when the child enters the activity, and they may refuse the child's requests to join an activity. Children who are socially rejected by some peers usually do not have any friends (Odom et al., 2006).

Children who establish reciprocal friendships during preschool often have better social and academic outcomes (Hartup, 2017). Children who are socially rejected tend to have poorer mental health and academic outcomes. (To read more about children's friendships, see Strain, Guralnick, & Walker, 2013.)

WHAT SKILLS ARE INVOLVED IN FORMING FRIENDSHIPS AND SOCIAL RELATIONSHIPS?

To develop friendships, children need many opportunities to interact successfully with their peers. These interactions can be simple, such as passing materials to the child sitting next to them during a small-group activity or a meal, or more complex and extended, such as working together on a cooperative art project. Teachers play an important role in planning and supporting these activities. Instruction to develop social relationships should occur every day and across all classroom areas and activities. The teacher's role in supporting positive social relationships is often a delicate balance between helping and stepping back. The teacher should facilitate children's interaction but not interfere or take over the situation.

Not only can teachers arrange the classroom environment to support positive social interactions but they can also teach their students skills that are key to positive relationships. These skills include but are not limited to

- Being aware of others
- Sharing
- Helping others
- Persisting or making efforts to maintain social interactions
- Organizing play with others
- Being able to enter play situations

- Giving compliments
- Negotiating
- Solving conflicts

As with all skills, friendship skills can be incorporated into the general curriculum, and teachers should identify friendship learning objectives for children who are struggling with peer interaction.

STRATEGIES TO PROMOTE FRIENDSHIPS AND SOCIAL RELATIONSHIPS

The teacher or the team may use the steps outlined in Chapter 4 to identify friendship learning objectives, plan the level of intervention, determine when and where to intervene, and evaluate the effects of intervention. As always, teams need to select the appropriate level of support, whether it is a curriculum modification, an embedded learning opportunity (ELO), or more explicit instruction, such as a child-focused instructional strategy (CFIS).

When making plans to support social relationships, it is important to make sure that the activities in the classroom provide multiple opportunities every day for social interactions. Some ways to do this include providing activities and materials that require more than one child to participate. Some materials lend themselves to more social interaction than others (e.g., playing ball games, dramatic play), but even seemingly solitary activities (e.g., puzzles, games on a tablet) can be arranged to require a social component. Another point to remember is that social skills instruction should be incorporated within activities that build on children's interests and experiences. In other words, if a child who is socially isolated enjoys playing in the block area and really dislikes art activities, teachers will be more successful in incorporating peers during block play. It is always a good idea to use preferred materials and activities to teach new skills (see Chapter 5 for more information about curriculum modifications).

Planned classroom activities can also incorporate social opportunities. For example, pairs or small groups of children can complete class jobs, be dismissed for recess, make murals, build sculptures, or write storybooks. Sometimes children who lack social skills have difficulty with more open-ended activities. The teacher can provide structure by using visual supports. In the dramatic play area, for example, a photo display can provide children with a play script to get them started.

Routine classroom activities can also be used to promote social relationships. One simple way to do this is to change children's songs, rhymes, or games by inserting a social term or encouraging interaction. These are called *group friendship activities* (Cooper & McEvoy, 1996). For example, a line from the Hokey Pokey might be changed from "put your left foot in" to "shake your neighbor's hand."

Teaching social skills is like learning skills from other domains. Good instruction requires assessment, planning, implementation with fidelity, and evaluation. The best instruction takes place in the environment where children will need to use the target skills, so social skill instruction should take place in the classroom, on the playground, and any other place where children interact. Children need extended and repeated interactions with peers to develop friendships and social relationships that last beyond the immediate teaching situation. Part of the team's planning involves ensuring repeated and successful social interactions in the classroom and on the playground. Teams should be mindful to target the outcomes that are important to children and families. For example, if participating in group activities is valued by the families, that skill should be taught directly in the classroom.

A number of interventions have been shown to be successful in teaching the skills that are related to developing friendships and engaging in positive social relationships (for reviews, see Brown & Conroy, 2011; Wong et al., 2015). One approach to teaching these social-emotional skills that aligns well with Building Blocks is the Pyramid Model (Hemmeter, Snyder, Fox, & Algina, 2016). This tiered model of instruction and support provides guidelines for teachers to create responsive learning environments for all children and then plan instructional strategies for individual children who require additional specialized instruction in this domain. The National Center for Pyramid Model Innovations (http://challengingbehavior.cbcs.usf.edu) provides additional resources on interventions that work. Young children also meet potential friends in their neighborhoods and communities. Table 10.1 provides more ideas for facilitating friendships and social relationships using the Building Blocks framework.

Table 10.1. Examples of strategies for facilitating friendships and social relationships using the Building Blocks framework

Building Block	Strategies
Child-focused instructional strategies (CFIS)	Systematically teach children to take turns with peers during a highly preferred activity.
	Teach children (peers) to invite children who are more reluctant to play and then be persistent using visuals to remind the children to "Stay, Play, and Talk" with their friends.
	Teach children to compliment a child before attempting to join an ongoing activity.
	Use direct instruction methods to teach children to answer questions from their peers during play activities.
	Teach specific play routines that include peers, such as playing with dolls or with cars and trucks.
	Teach children to take turns with their favorite toys so that they learn that they will get the toy back after their peer has a turn to play.
Embedded learning opportunities (ELOs)	Plan dramatic play activities with specific roles (e.g., grocer, shopper, shelf stocker); assign the roles.
	Include actions of friendship, such as exchanging hugs and high-fives, during songs, group meetings, or other planned activities.
	"Sabotage" a small-group art activity by putting out an insufficient amount of materials; encourage the children to problem-solve how to share the materials and take turns.
	Set up a special buddy center during free-choice time; have children play with special toys and games that require working with a partner or a buddy.
	Assign two children to complete a classroom job.
Curriculum modifications (CMs)	Provide materials and equipment that facilitate social interaction (e.g., wagon, puppets, board games).
	Carefully select the members of small groups to facilitate social interaction.
	Use visual supports to help children solve conflicts.
	Make transition times social occasions by pairing children.
	Have children share or pass materials at circle time and snack time.
	Use preferred activities (e.g., art, outdoor play) to teach new friendship skills.
High-quality early childhood environment	Provide opportunities for children to observe and interact with socially competent peers.
	Plan cooperative activities that require more than one child.
	Use behavior-specific praise to comment on children who are playing together.
	Use behavior-specific praise to comment on children who are working out a conflict in a positive manner.
	Set up the environment to encourage two or more children to work together on projects and activities.
	Provide both structured and unstructured play times.
	Read books and have class discussions about friendship, problem solving, and conflict resolution.

Nhan's team took another look at his current performance in the classroom and decided to do two things. First, when planning his special language instruction sessions, whether using ELOs or CFIS, the team decided to have peers participate in the session or learning opportunity. Second, they planned more social opportunities for Nhan by seating him next to preferred peers at snack time and circle time and by adding a preferred social activity during outdoor time. Since implementing these interventions, the team has noticed that Nhan is spending more time with some of his pals.

Mr. Alvarez decided to implement group friendship activities in his classroom. Every day at circle time, he does one activity in which children shake hands, give high-fives, or pass a toy around the circle. After he implemented these group friendship activities, he observed that more children were playing together at free-choice time, and no one was being rejected anymore. He was pleased by these results and impressed with how easy it was to implement this strategy. By being more intentional in his teaching, he helped the children develop healthier social relationships.

Chapter 11

Developmentally Appropriate Classroom Behavior

Grace Martin started off the school year with high hopes. Over the summer, she worked on her teaching certificate and participated in a weeklong workshop on positive behavioral interventions and support (PBIS) at a local university. What she learned made sense to her, although classroom management (as she always thought of it) had never been her strength. However, now it is November, and she is frustrated; the strategies they talked about in her workshop seem impossible to implement in her classroom, and she feels like she is spending too much time disciplining and not enough time teaching. She does not know where to start or who to turn to for help.

Drew, who has autism, enjoys school—once he is there. He seems to enjoy every activity at school once he is engaged in the activity. In fact, he does not like to stop any activity in which he is engaged, whether it is at home, school, or child care. When he is asked to stop one activity and move to another, he usually begins to have a tantrum. Often, his teachers and parents let him continue doing what he is doing, but when they require him to move on to the next activity, he often cries during the entire transition. Once he is settled at the new activity, he calms down and begins to participate in an appropriate manner. Drew's transition behavior is stressful for the children and adults in the classroom, and many children are beginning to avoid Drew because of it. His parents also report that this behavior is becoming more difficult to deal with at home and in the community. What strategies can help Drew, his parents, and his teachers to have more successful transitions?

Most young children, both with and without disabilities, demonstrate some behavior that is challenging to their teacher, parents, and other caregivers. Experimentation with rules, boundaries, and consequences is a typical part of child development. For some young children, however, learning how to use materials appropriately, follow directions, and interact with peers and adults in group settings can be very challenging. It is essential that children learn these developmentally appropriate classroom behaviors because they affect success in early childhood settings and in subsequent educational and community settings. Addressing challenging behaviors in the classroom is consistently one of the most requested topics for professional development among early childhood educators. Decreasing the number of challenging behaviors in classrooms also increases the amount of time teachers can devote to teaching new and desired skills and concepts. This topic aligns with the Head Start Early Learning Outcome Framework (U.S. DHHS, 2015) under the domain of Approaches to Learning. These standards state that by the age of 5 children should be able to follow a classroom routine, ask for assistance when necessary, and manage materials in the classroom. The idea of designing classrooms and instruction to support appropriate child behavior is also evident in the Guiding Principles of the Head Start Framework document. The belief that "Every child is unique and can succeed" (p. 3) reminds teachers that student failure is instructional failure and it is incumbent on classroom teams to make the changes necessary to ensure the success of every child.

This chapter provides some practical suggestions for supporting appropriate classroom behavior and decreasing challenging behaviors that interfere with children's participation in classroom and community settings (see Table 11.1).

As mentioned, testing limits and asserting one's independence are part of the maturation process; this chapter does not address the types of limit-testing behavior that is typical of young children. Rather, the strategies discussed here can be applied at the classroom level to prevent challenging behaviors and with individual children when a challenging behavior persists (e.g., Dunlap, Wilson, Strain, & Lee, 2013; Sutherland et al., 2018).

This chapter uses the term *challenging behavior* to refer to behavior that is persistent; that interferes with a child's participation in classroom, community, or home activities; and that is perceived by parents and teachers to be a problem. The strategies are based on many years of work with young children and the burgeoning research literature on positive behavioral intervention and support (PBIS).

POSITIVE BEHAVIORAL INTERVENTION AND SUPPORT

Positive behavioral intervention and support (PBIS) is a comprehensive approach focusing on facilitating appropriate behaviors while preventing and reducing challenging and stigmatizing behaviors (www.pbis.org). A major goal of PBIS is to facilitate participation in meaningful activities and inclusive settings. A fundamental tenet of PBIS is that challenging behaviors have a communicative function. In other words, when children demonstrate these behaviors, they are trying to communicate something. They may be asking for attention or asking to be left alone; they may be trying to obtain some materials or trying to tell someone else that they do not want to share the materials.

Table 11.1. Examples of strategies for supporting developmentally appropriate classroom behavior using the Building Blocks framework

Building Block	Strategies
Child-focused instructional strategies (CFIS)	If children do not have an effective communication system, teach them how to request and to make an appropriate form of protest. Teach children specific vocabulary to use in problem solving. Teach children to label emotional states and be able to provide positive solutions to potential problems. If a child is aggressive toward peers and the result of a functional behavioral assessment (FBA) suggests that he or she is attempting to gain their attention, teach the child a more appropriate way to get their attention (e.g., tapping the person on the shoulder). Teach children to use a solution chart, a visual support strategy that suggests alternative ways to solve problems.
Embedded learning opportunities (ELOs)	Use individual picture schedules and timers to help children stay engaged in center activities for a specified length of time. Systematically teach children how to request toys from peers to decrease grabbing and aggression. Systematically teach children problem-solving skills for times when peer conflicts can occur. Teach children to use words to label their emotional states when they are experiencing the emotion (e.g., happy, sad, mad, frustrated, anxious). Provide positive feedback and behavior specific for children who are participating in classroom activities and following classroom rules.
Curriculum modifications (CMs)	Assign seating for small-group activities and class meetings. Use picture schedules and other visual support strategies, including process charts that outline complex play activities. Use work mats and other strategies to help children define their own space. Limit the number of children in a center at one time to avoid crowding; use a check-in/check-out chart. Provide activities and materials in every center that appeal to the interest and abilities of the entire range of children in your classroom.
High-quality early childhood environment	Provide a clear and consistent classroom schedule. Establish a few simple classroom rules. Offer a well-designed environment, including clearly marked activity centers. Provide interesting, developmentally appropriate, and well-maintained materials. Include a variety and balance of activities, including activities for both active and quiet play.

The idea that challenging behaviors have a communicative function changes the approach to managing these behaviors. Rather than attempt to eliminate the behaviors immediately, teachers should understand what the child is trying to communicate and then teach the child a more appropriate way to accomplish his or her goal. This shifts the emphasis from adult-directed classroom management systems to more shared control between adult and child. It also emphasizes supporting the child's appropriate behavior while making sure that the inappropriate behavior is no longer effective in achieving the communicative goal. Therefore, an essential component to any positive support plan is to teach the child an appropriate alternative behavior. For example, if a child throws a puzzle because he or she needs help with it, the child needs to learn how to ask a teacher for help in addition to learning that throwing the puzzle is not acceptable. Or, if a child hits a teacher to get the teacher's attention, the child needs to learn how to tap the teacher gently on the arm to get his or her attention in addition to learning that hitting is not acceptable.

WHAT ARE DEVELOPMENTALLY APPROPRIATE CLASSROOM BEHAVIORS?

Developmentally appropriate classroom behaviors include the basic skills that most preschool children can demonstrate. They include but are not limited to

- Following simple directions given to an individual
- Following simple directions given to the group
- Making classroom transitions, including putting materials away
- Following basic classroom rules
- Regulating and expressing emotions in an appropriate manner
- Using appropriate and peaceful strategies to resolve conflicts with peers
- Stopping an inappropriate behavior when asked by an adult

When addressing challenging behaviors, it is always important to begin by identifying the appropriate alternative behavior, in other words the behavior that the child should be demonstrating. The teacher needs to consider what function the behavior serves for a child and how the child will be able to achieve that function in a more appropriate manner. For example, Drew's behavior during transitions may mean that he does not understand why he needs to stop one activity and that he does not know what the next activity will be. Drew's teachers and family could help Drew achieve this need for information by providing him with visual cues (e.g., pictures or symbols) for the transition.

A common and often very upsetting challenging behavior in preschool is aggression. Aggression includes hitting, kicking, pinching, throwing objects at people, and other types of unfriendly touching. Aggression is sometimes difficult for staff members to cope with because most people have preconceived, and often very strong, beliefs about how to deal with aggression in young children. Using a PBIS approach requires that teachers disregard their preconceived notions and address aggression systematically. Coping with children's aggression is a formidable task, especially when children are aggressive toward their peers, because school must be a safe place for all children. As one early childhood administrator tells parents in her center when asked about a child who demonstrates aggressive or dangerous behavior, "The behavior is unacceptable and must be eliminated, but the child is a member of our school and it is our job to teach him some more appropriate alternatives." The next section discusses how to teach appropriate behaviors that can take the place of those challenging behaviors.

TEACHING DEVELOPMENTALLY APPROPRIATE CLASSROOM BEHAVIORS

The Building Blocks framework, described throughout this book, offers an appropriate way to approach challenging behaviors. What is important about this approach is that it is not a one-size-fits-all way to handle behavior. It encourages teachers to work with the team, including the family, to provide the right amount of support and instruction to the child (e.g., Lucyshyn et al., 2015). When addressing challenging behaviors, teachers should begin by looking at the classroom environment (see the Quality Classroom Assessment Form in Appendix A). The classroom must provide appropriate activities, including a mix of active and quiet activities; an appropriate environment, including enough space and materials in good working order; and an appropriate level of structure, including a schedule, simple classroom rules, and a room with clearly defined centers.

Some children may need modifications to the physical or temporal environment and to the activities in the classroom. Many children, such as those who have difficulty with receptive language, may benefit from picture schedules or other visual cues, which help to decrease challenging behaviors during transitions and free-choice time. Other children may need additional visual reminders to help them participate more fully, such as work mats during art projects, carpet squares during circle time, or labels or symbols on containers to facilitate cleanup. Other children may need more explicit instruction to acquire appropriate alternative behaviors. For example, Drew needs explicit instruction to learn how to use the picture schedule and other visual supports, but once he learns the new routine, the visual supports will function like simple curriculum modifications. A child who demonstrates aggressive behavior may need repeated ELOs to learn how to share preferred materials without hitting. This type of intervention is not easy, but spending time with a child *before* the challenging behavior occurs can make teaching more effective and improve the entire classroom climate because the disruptive behavior is prevented. Two extremely helpful websites with a great deal of addition information on this topic are the National Center for Pyramid Model Innovations (http://challengingbehavior.cbcs.usf.edu/) and the Positive Behavioral Intervention and Supports Technical Assistance Center (https://www.pbis.org/).

When the team is deciding what type of intervention to use with a child, it is helpful to systematically collect information about the child and the behavior. The problem-solving framework provides a series of steps for collecting information that will lead to a potential solution for the problem (e.g., Dunlap et al., 2013; Koegel, Koegel, & Dunlap, 1996). Once you begin to use this framework to address challenging behaviors, you will realize that although many of the behaviors that occur in preschool classrooms are quickly resolved through intervention, others are not. It is important to monitor (i.e., collect data about) the child's behavior to make sure that the challenging behavior is decreasing. If it is not, you may need to reassess the behavior and try a different intervention.

All of the strategies described in this chapter can be used across settings and by different adults (e.g., Dunlap et al., 2016). For example, a visual schedule used to provide information to the child during transitions could also be used at home, child care, or Sunday school. Consistency across settings and adults is an important characteristic of any plan to teach children new, appropriate behaviors. When working with families to implement these strategies outside of the early learning program environment, it is important to ensure that behaviors being addressed are the behaviors that are most important for the families and that the child is learning an appropriate alternative behavior to use in place of the challenging behavior. Family members and other adults will also need training and coaching to help them learn when and how to implement these strategies accurately. An important part of a behavior change plan for any child demonstrating challenging behaviors should be frequent check-ins with the family. During these short meetings, teachers can share information about how the child is doing in the classroom (remember to report good news!) and inquire about how the child's behavior is outside of the early learning program.

PROBLEM-SOLVING FRAMEWORK FOR CHALLENGING BEHAVIORS

The following list outlines a system of addressing challenging behaviors in the classroom. This system includes the careful assessment, planning, and implementation of teaching plans that are used throughout the Building Blocks framework.

1. Define the challenging behavior.
2. Assess where and when the behavior is a problem.
3. Assess where and when the behavior is not a problem.
4. Assess what happens before and after the challenging behavior.
5. Assess classroom supports (e.g., adult, instructional, environmental).
6. Assess classroom barriers.
7. Determine what the child is attempting to communicate with the behavior.
8. Select an intervention.
9. Implement the intervention.
10. Monitor child behavior to ensure change.
11. Monitor the implementation to make sure that the adults are doing what they planned to do.

The system described here is similar to a *functional behavioral assessment* (FBA), which was first required by the Individuals with Disabilities Education Act Amendments of 1997 (PL 105-17) for children with challenging behaviors. The purpose of an FBA is to determine what function the behavior is serving for the child (Dunlap et al., 2013). In other words, an FBA attempts to determine what is motivating the behavior and what the child is communicating when he or she demonstrates the behavior. If the child with whom you are working has an IFSP or an IEP and demonstrates challenging behavior, you should conduct an FBA before you begin intervention. The representative from the school district is a key member of the team. This individual knows the district's procedures and can provide appropriate forms and assist with designing the FBA and subsequent intervention.

Grace decided that she was trying to do too many different things at once, and she felt that she was ignoring the basics of good planning and classroom arrangement. One afternoon, Grace and her team decided to use the Quality Classroom Assessment Form and make plans for changing two or three simple things. After reviewing their current practices, Grace and her team decided to implement the following three changes:

1. They developed a regular daily schedule and stuck to it. They also made a copy of the schedule with pictures and taught the children how to determine what the next activity would be.

2. They provided more choices during center time and limited the number of children in a center at any one time.
3. They increased the number of positive statements they made to children every day.

Making these changes was hard at first, but Grace is very proud of the results. After only 2 weeks, the children know the routine, and everyone in the classroom seems happier and calmer. Grace is excited and has already planned another staff meeting in a month to see if more changes are necessary.

After examining their situation, Drew's team thought the best way to proceed was to use a picture schedule in the classroom and help Drew attend to the pictures and follow through at each transition. After trying this for 2 weeks with no change in behavior, the team decided to do something different. They made Drew a series of transition cards using symbols the teacher downloaded from a web site. When it was time for a transition, the teacher simply put the appropriate symbol in Drew's hand and said, "Drew, it is time to go to circle." It worked! After only 1 week, Drew was making transitions with no problem. His teacher has made a set of these cards for home and the child care center to see if they help with his transition problems in those settings.

Chapter 12

Concluding Thoughts

Inclusion is about belonging and participating in a diverse society. Inclusive classrooms reflect the cultures, values, and beliefs of the communities in which they are located. The inclusion of young children with disabilities and other special needs in early childhood classrooms is not only supported by federal law and research, but it is a reality in our increasingly diverse communities. A substantial number of research studies report positive outcomes for children with and without disabilities in inclusive settings (Odom, Buysse, & Soukakou, 2011). Research also identifies some of the challenges and complexities of inclusion. One of the challenges is how to provide needed specialized instruction without interfering with the social ecology or curricular integrity of the inclusive classroom or early learning program.

The Building Blocks framework offers practical suggestions to help teachers accomplish this task. This book offers early childhood teachers practical and evidence-based strategies for including and teaching young children with special needs. Our aim is to help teachers make good, data-based decisions when selecting and using appropriate levels of assistance, working as teams, and using effective teaching strategies to help children attain important and worthwhile objectives.

Specialized instruction is an important component of inclusion. It is the cornerstone of special education. That is, a stated aim of education is to enhance young children's development and learning by teaching new skills, attempting to remediate delays, and preventing secondary disabilities. Instruction is intentional and evaluated. In fact, if the instruction being provided in any program is not helping the children learn, it is the responsibility of the educational team to make changes to that instruction. Effective instruction yields child success. At the same time, in the effort to enhance children's development and learning, teaching teams should remember that the early childhood curriculum is broad and that there are many important things for young children to learn during the early years. For example, children expand their communication skills and begin to learn about reading and writing. They learn to get along with others and make friends. They refine their physical abilities. They learn to solve problems. Always, the goal is to promote a positive attitude toward learning and life. Thus, teaching efforts in inclusive classrooms must focus on the whole child and demonstrate appreciation of all of these important areas of learning.

Inclusion is not simply about children's social experiences. One of the repeated findings of the inclusion research is that just being in the general education classroom is not sufficient. There are critical features that are necessary for any child's early learning experiences. His or her development must be nurtured. Experiences must be developmentally appropriate and individually planned. The child must be supported so that he or she may take advantage of the full complement of learning experiences. Instruction must be tailored to address individual needs and the effects of the instruction must be evaluated to ensure that the child is making meaningful progress.

The Building Blocks framework recognizes that it is difficult to provide individualized, specialized instruction in busy, action-packed classrooms and early learning programs. It takes planning and attention. The framework provides teachers with a range of supports and instruction to make inclusion successful and rewarding for everyone. Successful teaching results in children learning the valuable skills and concepts identified for them and being able to use them in meaningful ways. Successful teaching means that children will learn and thrive in your classroom, in their homes, and in their communities.

References

Allen, K. E., Hart, B., Buell, J. S., Harris, F. T., & Wolf, M. M. (1964). Effects of social reinforcement on isolate behavior of a nursery school child. *Child Development, 35*(2), 511–518.

Americans with Disabilities Act (ADA) of 1990, PL 101-336, 42 U.S.C. §§ 12101 *et seq.*

Azrin, N., & Foxx, R. (1989). *Toilet training in less than a day.* New York, NY: Pocket Books.

Baker, B. L., & Brightman, A. J. (with Blacher, J. B., Heifetz, L. J., Hinshaw, S. P., & Murphy, D. M.) (2004). *Steps to independence: Teaching everyday skills to children with special needs* (4th ed.). Baltimore, MD: Paul H. Brookes Publishing Co.

Barnett, W. S., Jung, K., Wong, V., Cook, T., & Lamy, C. (2007). *Effects of five state prekindergarten programs on early learning.* Retrieved from http://citeseerx.ist.psu.edu/viewdoc/download?doi=10.1.1.494.8287&rep=rep1&type=pdf

Barton, E. E., & Smith, B. J. (2015). *The preschool inclusion toolbox: How to build and lead a high-quality program.* Baltimore, MD: Paul H. Brookes Publishing Co.

Berrueta-Clement, J. R., Schweinhart, L. J., Barnett, S. W., Epstein, A. S., & Weikart, D. P. (1984). *Changed lives: The effects of the Perry Preschool Program on youths through age 19.* Ypsilanti, MI: High/Scope Press.

Bricker, D. (Series ed.). (2019). *Assessment, Evaluation, and Programming System (AEPS®) for Infants and Children* (2nd ed.). Baltimore, MD: Paul H. Brookes Publishing Co.

Brown, E. D., Benedett, B., & Armistead, M. E. (2010). Arts enrichment and school readiness for children at risk. *Early Childhood Research Quarterly, 25*(1), 112–124.

Brown, E. D., & Sax, K. L. (2013). Arts enrichment and preschool emotions for low-income children at risk. *Early Childhood Research Quarterly, 28*(2), 337–346.

Brown, W. H., & Conroy, M. A. (2011). Social-emotional competence in young children with developmental delays: Our reflection and vision for the future. *Journal of Early Intervention, 33*(4), 310–320.

Buysse, V., Goldman, B. D., West, T., & Hollingsworth, H. (2008). Friendships in early childhood: Implications for early education and intervention. In W. H. Brown, S. L. Odom, & S. R. McConnell (Eds.), *Social competence of young children: Risk, disability, and intervention* (pp. 77–97). Baltimore, MD: Paul H. Brookes Publishing Co.

Buysse, V., & Peisner-Feinberg, E. S. (Eds.). (2013). *Handbook of response to intervention in early childhood.* Baltimore, MD: Paul H. Brookes Publishing Co.

Carle, E. (1967). *Brown bear, brown bear, what do you see?* New York, NY: Doubleday.

Carle, E. (1969). *The very hungry caterpillar.* New York, NY: Philomel.

Carta, J. J., Sainato, D. M., & Greenwood, C. R. (1988). Advances in the ecological assessment of classroom instruction for young children with handicaps. In S. L. Odom & M. B. Karnes (Eds.), *Early intervention for infants and children with handicaps: An empirical base* (pp. 217–239). Baltimore, MD: Paul H. Brookes Publishing Co.

Collins, G. C. (2012). *Systematic instruction for students with moderate and severe disabilities.* Baltimore, MD: Paul H. Brookes Publishing Co.

Cooper, C. S., & McEvoy, M. A. (1996). Group friendship activities: An easy way to develop the social skills of young children. *Teaching Exceptional Children, 28*(3), 67–69.

Copple, C., & Bredekamp, S. (2009). *Developmentally appropriate practice in early childhood programs serving children from birth through age 8* (3rd ed.). Washington, DC: National Association for the Education of Young Children.

Cost, Quality, and Child Outcomes Study Team. (1995). *The study of cost, quality, and child outcomes in child care centers.* Denver: Department of Economics, University of Colorado at Denver.

Daugherty, S., Grisham-Brown, J., & Hemmeter, M. L. (2001). The effects of embedded skill instruction on the acquisition of target and nontarget skills in preschoolers with developmental delays. *Topics in Early Childhood Special Education, 21,* 214–221.

de la Peña, M. (2015). *Last stop on Market Street.* New York, NY: G.P. Putnam's Sons Books for Young Readers.

Diamond, A., & Lee, K. (2011). Interventions shown to aid executive function development in children 4 to 12 years old. *Science, 333*(6045), 959–964.

Division for Early Childhood. (2014). *DEC recommended practices in early intervention/early childhood special education 2014*. Retrieved from http://www.dec-sped.org/recommendedpractices

Division for Early Childhood/National Association for the Education of Young Children. (2009). *Early childhood inclusion: A joint position statement of the Division for Early Childhood (DEC) and the National Association for the Education of Young Children (NAEYC)*. Chapel Hill: The University of North Carolina, FPG Child Development Institute.

Dodge, D. T. (2010). *The Creative Curriculum for Preschool* (5th ed.). Washington, DC: Teaching Strategies.

Dodge, D. T., Rudick, S., & Berke, K. (2006). *The Creative Curriculum for Infants, Toddlers & Twos* (2nd ed.). Washington, DC: Teaching Strategies.

Dunlap, G., Fox, L., Lee, J. K., Strain, P. S., Vatland, C., Joseph, J. D., & Turnbull, A. (2016). *Prevent-Teach-Reinforce for families: A model of individualized positive behavior support for home and community*. Baltimore, MD: Paul H. Brookes Publishing Co.

Dunlap, G., Wilson, K., Strain, P., & Lee J. K. (2013). *Prevent-Teach-Reinforce for young children*. Baltimore, MD: Paul H. Brookes Publishing Co.

Early Childhood Technical Assistance Center. (n.d.). *Outcomes*. Retrieved from http://ectacenter.org/outcomes.asp

Eastman, P. D. (1961). *Go, dog, go!* New York, NY: Random House.

Emberley, E. (1992). *Go away, big green monster!* Boston, MA: Little, Brown.

Epstein, A., Hohmann, M., & HighScope Educational Research Foundation. (2012). *The HighScope Preschool Curriculum*. Ypsilanti, MI: High/Scope Press.

Every Student Succeeds Act of 2015, PL 114-95, 20 U.S.C. §§ 1400 *et seq.*

Farran, D. C., Lipsey, M. W., Watson, B., & Hurley, S. (2007). *Balance of content emphasis and child content engagement in an Early Reading First program*. Paper presented at the American Educational Research Association, Chicago, IL.

Fowler, S. A., Dougherty, B. S., Kirby, K. C., & Kohler, F. W. (1986). Role reversals: An analysis of therapeutic effects achieved with disruptive boys during their appointments as peer monitors. *Journal of Applied Behavior Analysis, 19*(4), 437–444.

Friend, M., & Cook, L. (2013). *Interactions: Collaboration skills for school professionals* (7th ed.). Boston, MA: Pearson.

Fuson, K. C., Clements, D. H., & Sarama, J. (2015). Making early math education work for all children. *Phi Delta Kappan, 97*(3), 63–68.

Gauvreau, A., & Sandall, S. R. (2018). Activity matrices: Tools for planning, organizing and implementing instruction in early childhood settings. In P. A. Snyder & M. L. Hemmeter (Eds.), *Instruction: Effective strategies to support engagement, learning, and outcomes* (DEC Recommended Practices Monograph Series No. 4) (pp. 37–50). Washington, DC: Division for Early Childhood.

Giangreco, M., Dennis, R., Edelman, S., & Cloninger, C. (1994). Dressing your IEPs for the general education climate: Analysis of IEP goals and objectives for students with multiple disabilities. *Remedial and Special Education, 15*, 288–326.

Goldstein, H., Lackey, K. C., & Schneider, N. J. (2014). A new framework for systematic reviews: Application to social skills interventions for preschoolers with autism. *Exceptional Children, 80*(3), 262–286.

Grisham-Brown, J., & Hemmeter, M. L. (2017). *Blended practices for teaching young children in inclusive settings*. Baltimore, MD: Paul H. Brookes Publishing Co.

Hamre, B. K., LaParo, K., Pianta, R. C., & LoCasale-Crouch, J. (2014). *Classroom Assessment Scoring System (CLASS) manual, infant*. Baltimore, MD: Paul H. Brookes Publishing Co.

Hamre, B. K., & Pianta, R. C. (2005). Can instructional and emotional support in the first-grade classroom make a difference for children at risk of school failure. *Child Development, 76*(5), 949–967.

Harms, T., Clifford, R. M., & Cryer, D. (2015). *Early Childhood Environment Rating Scale* (3rd ed.). New York, NY: Teachers College Press.

Harms, T., Cryer, D., & Clifford, R. M. (2007). *Family Child Care Environment Rating Scale* (Rev. ed.). New York, NY: Teachers College Press.

Harms, T., Cryer, D., Clifford, R. M., & Yazejian, N. M. (2017). *Infant/Toddler Environment Rating Scale* (3rd ed.). New York, NY: Teachers College Press.

Hart, B., & Risley, T. R. (1975). Incidental teaching of language in the preschool. *Journal of Applied Behavior Analysis, 8*, 411–420.

Hart, B., & Risley, T. R. (1995). *Meaningful differences in the everyday experience of young American children*. Baltimore, MD: Paul H. Brookes Publishing Co.

Hartup, W. W. (2017). Children and their friends. In H. McGurk (Ed.), *Issues in childhood social development* (pp. 130–170). London, UK: Routledge.

Hemmeter, M. L., Snyder, P. A., Fox, L., & Algina, J. (2016). Evaluating the implementation of the Pyramid Model for promoting social-emotional competence in early childhood classrooms. *Topics in Early Childhood Special Education, 36*(3), 133–146.

Hepting, N. H., & Goldstein, H. (1996). What's natural about naturalistic language intervention? *Journal of Early Intervention, 20*, 249–265.

Heroman, C., Tabors, P. O., & Teaching Strategies, Inc. (2010). *Teaching Strategies GOLD: Birth through Kindergarten: Assessment toolkit.* Washington, DC: Teaching Strategies.

HighScope Educational Research Foundation. (2015). *Child Observation Record (COR) Advantage.* Ypsilanti, MI: High/Scope Press.

Hintz, A., & Smith, A. T. (2013). Mathematizing read-alouds in three easy steps. *The Reading Teacher, 67*(2), 103–108.

Horn, E., & Banerjee, R. (2009). Understanding curriculum modifications and embedded learning opportunities in the context of supporting all children's success. *Language, Speech, and Hearing Services in Schools, 40*, 406–415.

Horn, E., Lieber, J., Li, S. M., Sandall, S. R., & Schwartz, I. S. (2000). Supporting young children's IEP goals in inclusive settings through embedded learning opportunities. *Topics in Early Childhood Special Education, 20*, 208–223.

Horn, E., Lieber, J., Sandall, S. R., Schwartz, I. S., & Wolery, R. A. (2001). Classroom models of individualized instruction. In S. L. Odom (Ed.), *Widening the circle: Including children with disabilities in preschool programs* (pp. 46–60). New York, NY: Teachers College Press.

Individuals with Disabilities Education Act Amendments of 1997, PL 105-17, 20 U.S.C. §§ 1400 *et seq.*

Individuals with Disabilities Education Improvement Act of 2004, PL 108-446, 20 U.S.C. §§ 1400 *et seq.*

Koegel, L. K., Koegel, R. L., & Dunlap, G. (Eds.). (1996). *Positive behavioral support: Including people with difficult behavior in the community.* Baltimore, MD: Paul H. Brookes Publishing Co.

LaParo, K. M., Hamre, B. K., & Pianta, R. C. (2012). *Classroom Assessment Scoring System (CLASS) manual, toddler.* Baltimore, MD: Paul H. Brookes Publishing Co.

Lieber, J., Beckman, P. J., Hanson, M. J., Sando, S., Marquart, J. M., Horn, E. M., & Odom, S. L. (1997). The impact of changing roles on relationships between professionals in inclusive programs for young children. *Early Education and Development, 8*, 67–83.

Lobo, Y. B., & Winsler, A. (2006). The effects of a creative dance and movement program on the social competence of Head Start preschoolers. *Social Development, 15*(3), 501–519.

Lucyshyn, J., Fossett, B., Bakeman, R., Cheremshynski, C., Miller, L., Lohrmann, S., . . . Irvin, L. (2015). Transforming parent–child interaction in family routines: Longitudinal analysis with families of children with developmental disabilities. *Journal of Child and Family Studies, 24*(12), 3526–3541.

McBride, B. J., & Schwartz, I. S. (2003). Effects of teaching early interventionists to use discrete trials during ongoing classroom activities. *Topics in Early Childhood Special Education, 23*, 5–17.

McClelland, M. M., & Cameron, C. E. (2018). Developing together: The role of executive function and motor skills in children's early academic lives. *Early Childhood Research Quarterly.* https://doi.org/10.1016/j.ecresq.2018.03.014

McCormick, L., & Feeney, S. (1995). Modifying and expanding activities for children with disabilities. *Young Children, 50*(4), 10–17.

Meyer, A., Rose, D. H., & Gordon, D. (2014). *Universal design for learning: Theory and practice.* Wakefield, MA: CAST Professional Publishing.

Moomaw, S., & Davis, A. (2010). STEM comes to preschool. *Young Children, 65*(5), 12–14.

National Association for the Education of Young Children & National Association of Early Childhood Specialists in State Departments of Education (2003). *Early childhood curriculum, assessment, and program evaluation.* Retrieved from https://www.naeyc.org/sites/default/files/globally-shared/downloads/PDFs/resources/position-statements/pscape.pdf

National Association for the Education of Young Children (NAEYC). (2001). *10 signs of a great preschool.* Retrieved from http://oldweb.naeyc.org/ece/1996/01.asp

National Professional Development Center on Inclusion. (2009). *Research synthesis points on quality inclusive practices.* Retrieved from https://npdci.fpg.unc.edu/sites/npdci.fpg.unc.edu/files/resources/NPDCI-ResearchSynthesisPointsInclusivePractices-2011_0.pdf

No Child Left Behind Act of 2001, PL 107-110, 115 Stat. 1425, 20 U.S.C. §§ 6301 *et seq.*

Odom, S. L. (Ed.). (2001). *Widening the circle: Including children with disabilities in preschool programs.* New York, NY: Teachers College Press.

Odom, S. L., Buysse, V., & Soukakou, E. (2011). Inclusion for young children with disabilities: A quarter century of research perspectives. *Journal of Early Intervention, 33*, 344–356.

Odom, S. L., Horn, E. M., Marquart, J. M., Hanson, M. J., Wolfberg, P., Beckman, P., . . . Sandall, S. (1999). On the forms of inclusion: Organizational context and individualized service models. *Journal of Early Intervention, 22*, 185–199.

Odom, S. L., Zercher, C., Li, S., Marquart, J. M., Sandall, S. R., & Brown, W. H. (2006). Social acceptance and rejection of preschool children with disabilities: A mixed-method analysis. *Journal of Educational Psychology, 98,* 807–832.

Peisner-Feinberg, E. S., Burchinal, M. R., Clifford, R. M., Culkin, M. L., Howes, C., Kagain, S. L., . . . Rusticl, J. (1999). *The children of the Cost, Quality and Outcomes Study go to school: Technical report.* Chapel Hill: University of North Carolina at Chapel Hill, Frank Porter Graham Child Development Center.

Phillips, B., & Halle, J. (2004). The effects of a teacher-training intervention on student interns' use of naturalistic language teaching strategies. *Teacher Education and Special Education, 27,* 81–96.

Pianta, R. C., LaParo, K. M., & Hamre, B. K. (2008). *Classroom Assessment Scoring System* (CLASS). Baltimore, MD: Paul H. Brookes Publishing Co.

Ramey, C. T., Campbell, F. A., Burchinal, M., Skinner, M. L., Gardner, D. M., & Ramey, S. L. (2000). Persistent effects of early intervention on high-risk children and their mothers. *Applied Developmental Science, 4,* 2–14.

Rehabilitation Act of 1973, PL 93-112, 29 U.S.C. §§ 701 *et seq.*

Ritblatt, S., Longstreth, S., Hokoda, A., Cannon, B. N., & Weston, J. (2013). Can music enhance school-readiness socioemotional skills? *Journal of Research in Childhood Education, 27*(3), 257–266.

Rule, S., Losardo, A., Dinnebeil, L. A., Kaiser, A., & Rowland C. (1998). Research challenges in naturalistic intervention. *Journal of Early Intervention, 21,* 283–293.

Sadao, K. C., & Robinson, N. B. (2010). *Assistive technology for young children: Creating inclusive learning environments.* Baltimore, MD: Paul H. Brookes Publishing Co.

Sainato, D. M., Strain, P. S., Lefebvre, D., & Rapp, N. (1990). Effects of self-evaluation on the independent work skills of preschool children with disabilities. *Exceptional Children, 56,* 540–549.

Sandall, S. R., Hemmeter, M. L., Smith, B. J., & McLean, M. (2005). *DEC Recommended Practices: A comprehensive guide for practical application in early intervention/early childhood special education.* Longmont, CO: Sopris West Educational Services.

Sandall, S. R., & Schwartz, I. S. (2013). Building Blocks: A framework for meeting the needs of all children. In V. Buysse & E. S. Peisner-Feinberg (Eds.), *Handbook of response to intervention in early childhood* (pp. 103–120). Baltimore, MD: Paul H. Brookes Publishing Co.

Sandall, S. R., Schwartz, I. S., & Gauvreau, A. (2016). Using modifications and accommodations to enhance learning of young children with disabilities: Little changes that yield big impacts. In B. Reichow, B. A. Boyd, E. E. Barton, & S. L. Odom (Eds.), *Handbook of early childhood special education* (pp. 349-361). New York, NY: Springer.

Schatschneider, C., Fletcher, J. M., Francis, D. J., Carlson, C. D., & Foorman, B. R. (2004). Kindergarten prediction of reading skills: A longitudinal comparative analysis. *Journal of Educational Psychology, 96*(2), 265.

Schwartz, I., Ashmun, J., McBride, B., Scott, C., & Sandall, S. R. (2017). *The DATA model for teaching preschoolers with autism.* Baltimore, MD: Paul H. Brookes Publishing Co.

Schwartz, I. S., Garfinkle, A., & Davis, C. (2002). Arranging preschool environments to facilitate valued social and educational outcomes. In M. Shinn, H. Walker, & G. Stoner (Eds.), *Interventions for academic and behavior problems II: Preventive and remedial approaches.* Bethesda, MD: National Association of School Psychologists.

Schwartz, I. S., & McBride, B. (2014). Getting a good start: Effective practices in early intervention. In K. D. Burton & P. Wolfberg (Eds.), *Educating learners on the autism spectrum: Preparing highly qualified educators and related practitioners* (2nd ed., pp. 82–105). Kansas City, KS: Autism Asperger Publishing.

Schweinhart, L. J., Barnes, H. V., & Weikart, D. P. (1993). *Significant benefits: The High/Scope Perry Preschool Study through age 27.* Ypsilanti, MI: High/Scope Press.

Simmons, D. C., Fuchs, L. S., Fuchs, D., Mathes, P., & Hodge, J. P. (1995). Effects of explicit teaching and peer tutoring on the reading achievement of learning-disabled and low-performing students in regular classrooms. *The Elementary School Journal, 95,* 387–409.

Snyder, P., Hemmeter, M. L., McLean, M. E., Sandall, S. R., McLaughlin, T., & Algina, J. (2018). Impact of professional development in preschool teachers' use of embedded instructional practices. *Exceptional Children, 84*(2), 213–232.

Snyder, P. A., Rakap, S., Hemmeter, M. L., McLaughlin, T. W., Sandall, S., & McLean, M. E. (2015). Naturalistic instructional approaches in early learning: A systematic review. *Journal of Early Intervention, 37*(1), 69–97.

Soanes, C. (Ed.). (2009). *Oxford dictionary of current English* (4th ed.). New York, NY: Oxford University Press.

Soukakou, E. (2016). *The Inclusive Classroom Profile.* Baltimore, MD: Paul H. Brookes Publishing Co.

Strain, P. S., & Bovey, E. H. (2011). Randomized, controlled trial of the LEAP model of early intervention for young children with autism spectrum disorders. *Topics in Early Childhood Special Education, 31,* 133–154.

Strain, P. S., Guralnick, M. J., & Walker, H. M. (Eds.). (2013). *Children's social behavior: Development, assessment, and modification.* New York, NY: Elsevier.

Strain, P. S., & Hoyson, M. (2000). The need for longitudinal, intensive social skill intervention: LEAP follow-up outcomes for children with autism. *Topics in Early Childhood Special Education, 20,* 116–122.

Strain, P. S., Kerr, M. M., & Ragland, E. U. (1979). Effects of peer-mediated social initiations and prompting/reinforcement procedures on the social behavior of autistic children. *Journal of Autism and Developmental Disorders, 9,* 41–54.

Sutherland, K. S., Conroy, M. A., Algina, J., Ladwig, C., Jessee, G., & Gyure, M. (2018). Reducing child problem behaviors and improving teacher–child interactions and relationships: A randomized controlled trial of BEST in CLASS. *Early Childhood Research Quarterly, 42,* 31–43.

Trivette, C. M., Dunst, C. J., Hamby, D. W., & O'Herin, C. E. (2010). Effects of different types of adaptations on the behavior of young children with disabilities. *Research Brief, 4*(1). Tots-n-Tech Institute. Retrieved from https://www.ctdinstitute.org/sites/default/files/file_attachments/TnT-RB-V4.1-2010-Effects-of-adaptations-on-behavior.pdf

U.S. Department of Health and Human Services, Administration for Children and Families, Office of Head Start. (2015). *Head Start Early Learning Outcomes Framework: Ages birth to five.* Retrieved from https://eclkc.ohs.acf.hhs.gov/sites/default/files/pdf/elof-ohs-framework.pdf

Weikart, D. P., Bond, J. T., & McNeil, J. T. (1978). The Ypsilanti Perry Preschool Project: Preschool years and longitudinal results through fourth grade. *Monographs of the High/Scope Educational Research Foundation* (Vol. 3). Ypsilanti, MI: High/Scope Press.

Wolery, M. (2005). DEC recommended practices: Child-focused practices. In S. Sandall, M. L. Hemmeter, B. J. Smith, & M. E. McLean (Eds.), *DEC recommended practices: A comprehensive guide for practical application in early intervention/early childhood special education* (pp. 71–106). Longmont, CO: Sopris West Educational Services.

Wolery, M., Anthony, L., Caldwell, N. K., Snyder, E. D., & Morgante, J. D. (2002). Embedding and distributing constant time delay in circle time and transitions. *Topics in Early Childhood Special Education, 22,* 14–25.

Wolery, M., Schroeder, C., Martin, C. G., Venn, M. L., Holcombe, A., Brookfield, J., . . . Flening, L. A. (1994). Classroom activities and areas: Regularity of use and perceptions of adaptability by general early educators. *Early Education and Development, 5*(3), 181-194.

Wong, C., Odom, S. L., Hume, K. A., Cox, A. W., Fettig, A., Kucharczyk, S., . . . Schultz, T. R. (2015). Evidence-based practices for children, youth, and young adults with autism spectrum disorder: A comprehensive review. *Journal of Autism and Developmental Disorders, 45*(7), 1951–1966.

Wood, A. (2000). *The napping house.* New York, NY: Harcourt Children's Books.

Yoshikawa, H., Weiland, C., Brooks-Gunn, J., Burchinal, M., Espinosa, L., Gormley, W. T., . . . Zaslow, M. (2013, October). *Investing in our future: The evidence base on preschool.* Washington, DC: Society for Research in Child Development. Retrieved from https://www.fcd-us.org/the-evidence-base-on-preschool/

Zelazo, P. D., Blair, C. B., & Willoughby, M. T. (2016). *Executive function: Implications for education* (NCER 2017-2000). Washington, DC: U.S. Department of Education, National Center for Education Research, Institute of Education Sciences. Retrieved from http://ies.ed.gov/

Appendix A

Blank Forms

Quality Classroom Assessment Form

Classroom Action Worksheet

Child Assessment Worksheet

Planning Worksheet: Section I

Planning Worksheet: Section II

Child Activity Matrix

Classroom Activity Matrix

Evaluation Worksheet

ELO-at-a-Glance

Instruction-at-a-Glance

Checklist for Important Elements for Supporting Early Literacy

Quality Classroom Assessment Form

Date: ______________________

Classroom: ____

Team members: ______________________ ______________________

______________________ ______________________

Goal: ____

Indicator	Yes	No	Not sure	Examples
1. Do children spend most of their time playing and working with materials or with other children?				
2. Do children have access to various activities throughout the day?				
3. Do teachers work with individual children, small groups, and the whole group at different times during the day?				
4. Is the classroom decorated with children's original artwork, their own writing, and stories they've dictated?				
5. Do children learn within meaningful (i.e., relevant to their interests and experiences) contexts?				

(continued)

Quality Classroom Assessment Form

(continued)

Indicator	Yes	No	Not sure	Examples
6. Do children work on projects and have periods of time to play and explore?				
7. Do children have an opportunity to play and explore outside every day?				
8. Do teachers read books to children individually or in small groups throughout the day?				
9. Is the curriculum adapted for those who are ahead as well as those who need additional help?				
10. Do the children and their families feel safe and secure within their early childhood program?				

Notes: ____

____

____

____

Classroom Action Worksheet

Date: ______________________

Team members: ____

Indicator*	What's the problem?	What can we do?	Who will do it?	By when?

* Abbreviated from Quality Classroom Assessment Form.

Child Assessment Worksheet

Date: ______________________

Teacher's name: ______________________ Child's name: ______________________

Classroom activities	Classroom expectations	Child's level of performance
		Strength ______ Average ______ Area of concern ______
		Strength ______ Average ______ Area of concern ______
		Strength ______ Average ______ Area of concern ______
		Strength ______ Average ______ Area of concern ______

(continued)

Child Assessment Worksheet

(continued)

Date: ______________________

Teacher's name: ______________________ Child's name: ______________________

Classroom activities	Classroom expectations	Child's level of performance
		Strength ______ Average ______ Area of concern ______
		Strength ______ Average ______ Area of concern ______
		Strength ______ Average ______ Area of concern ______
		Strength ______ Average ______ Area of concern ______

Planning Worksheet: Section I

IEP Today

Date: ______________________________

Teacher's name: ______________________________ Child's name: ______________________________

The "IEP Today" is based on the child's complete individualized education program (IEP) and tells the team the child's individual goals and the associated objectives that are the current focus of instruction.

Goal/domain	Current objective(s)

(continued)

Planning Worksheet: Section II

Date: ______________________

Teacher's name: ______________________ Child's name: ______________________

This planning guide will help you collect more specific information for areas of concern for specific children. Using the Child Assessment Worksheet, identify three activities on which you would like to focus your attention. Once you identify the problem, collecting information is the next for instructional planning for children in inclusive settings.

Key: CM = curriculum modification; ELO = embedded learning opportunity; CFIS = child-focused instructional strategy.

Activities	Define concern	What are you currently doing?	Ideas for instruction
			CM ____ ELO ____ CFIS ____ Describe:
			CM ____ ELO ____ CFIS ____ Describe:
			CM ____ ELO ____ CFIS ____ Describe:

Child Activity Matrix

Date: ______________________

Teacher's name: ______________________ Child's name: ______________________

Write the classroom schedule in the left-hand column. Write the child's current learning objectives across the top row. Fill in the appropriate cells with brief versions of the selected teaching strategy.

Key: CM = curriculum modification; ELO = embedded learning opportunity; CFIS = child-focused instructional strategy.

Classroom Activity Matrix

Date: ______________________ Teacher's name: ______________________

Write the children's names across the top row. Write the classroom schedule in the left-hand column, starting with the second row. Fill in the appropriate cells with brief versions of the selected teaching strategy.

Key: CM = curriculum modification; ELO = embedded learning opportunity; CFIS = child-focused instructional strategy.

Evaluation Worksheet

Date: ______________________

Teacher's name: ______________________ Child's name: ______________________

Concern	Plan	Evaluation information
		Counts ______ Notes ______ Products ______ Did the plan work? Yes No What will you do next week?
		Counts ______ Notes ______ Products ______ Did the plan work? Yes No What will you do next week?
		Counts ______ Notes ______ Products ______ Did the plan work? Yes No What will you do next week?

ELO-at-a-Glance

Date: ____________________

Team members: ____________________ ____________________

____________________ ____________________

Child's name: ____________________

Routines: ____________________

Objective: ____________________

____

What are you going to do?

What are you going to say?

How will you respond?

What materials do you need?

How many opportunities will you provide each day?

Monday	Tuesday	Wednesday	Thursday	Friday

Instruction-at-a-Glance

Date: ______________________

Child's name: ________________ Teacher's name: ________________

Objective: ____

____

1. Setting for instruction

   When? ____

   Where? ____

   How often? ____________________________________

   Materials needed? ______________________________

2. Instructional interaction

Antecedent	Child behavior	Consequence
Instruction		Positive reinforcement
Prompt		Corrective feedback

(continued)

Instruction-at-a-Glance

(continued)

3. Monitoring progress:

Instructions: For the numbers 5–0 and ND ("No data") in the columns representing number of trials, circle or draw a line through each number, depending on response: ◯ = correct, ⁄ = incorrect.

Date

Current step														
	5	5	5	5	5	5	5	5	5	5	5	5	5	5
	4	4	4	4	4	4	4	4	4	4	4	4	4	4
	3	3	3	3	3	3	3	3	3	3	3	3	3	3
	2	2	2	2	2	2	2	2	2	2	2	2	2	2
	1	1	1	1	1	1	1	1	1	1	1	1	1	1
	0	0	0	0	0	0	0	0	0	0	0	0	0	0
Criteria:	ND	ND	ND	ND	ND	ND	ND	ND	ND	ND	ND	ND	ND	ND

4. Comments, questions, or issues to discuss with the team:

Checklist of Important Elements for Supporting Early Literacy

Availability of learning materials	___ At least five picture books per child ___ Three-dimensional alphabet letters ___ Variety of writing implements (crayons, pencils, markers, colored pencils) and paper ___ Games, materials, and activities to help children learn to name and print alphabet letters ___ Games, materials, and activities to help children learn to rhyme ___ Cozy and comfortable area where children can look at books of their own choice ___ Separate area with table or other surface readily available for writing
Availability of early literacy learning opportunities	___ Adults read aloud to children at least once a day ___ Teacher introduces new words to children while reading picture books ___ Teacher sometimes sounds out printed words when reading picture books and sometimes points to text while reading aloud ___ Teacher encourages children to scribble and experiment with pretend writing ___ Teacher has detailed and informative conversations with children about things that interest them (e.g., "How do you think ice cream is made?") ___ Teacher encourages children to talk about their experiences ___ Teacher helps children learn nursery rhymes ___ Teacher encourages children to express themselves using complete sentences ___ Teacher keeps a record of how individual children are progressing in their early literacy learning ___ Teacher believes in the importance of helping young children gain early literacy knowledge ___ Teacher engages children in games and activities that focus on phonological awareness (e.g., "Clap your hands for every sound you hear in *po-ta-to*") ___ Teacher helps children learn to write their own and others' names ___ Teacher regularly helps children learn the sounds the alphabet letters represent (e.g., "*M* makes the *mmmm* sound") ___ Classroom day includes some planned teaching activities in which all children are expected to engage in literacy activities

Appendix B

Additional Resources

GENERAL EARLY CHILDHOOD EDUCATION

Bohart, H., Charner, K., & Koralek, D. G. (Eds.). (2015). *Spotlight on young children: Exploring play.* Washington, DC: National Association for the Education of Young Children.

Bowman, B. T., Donovan, M. S., & Burns, M. S. (2000). *Eager to learn: Educating our preschoolers.* Washington, DC: National Academies Press.

Bredekamp, S. (in press). *Effective practices in early childhood education: Building a foundation* (4th ed.). Upper Saddle River, NJ: Pearson. (available 2019)

Copple, C., & Bredekamp, S. (2008). *Developmentally appropriate practice in early childhood from birth through age 8* (3rd ed.). Washington, DC: National Association for the Education of Young Children.

Division for Early Childhood. (2014). *DEC recommended practices in early intervention/ early childhood special education 2014.* Retrieved from http://www.dec-sped.org /recommendedpractices

Dombro, A. L., Stetson, C., & Jablon, J. (2011). *Powerful interactions: How to connect with children to extend their learning.* Washington, DC: National Association for the Education of Young Children.

Epstein, A. S. (2014). *The intentional teacher: Choosing the best strategies for young children's learning.* Washington, DC: National Association for the Education of Young Children.

INCLUSION

Barton, E. E., & Smith, B. J. (2015). *The preschool inclusion toolbox: How to build and lead a high-quality program.* Baltimore, MD: Paul H. Brookes Publishing Co.

Division for Early Childhood/National Association for the Education of Young Children. (2009). *Early childhood inclusion: A joint position statement of the Division for Early Childhood (DEC) and the National Association for the Education of Young Children (NAEYC).* Chapel Hill: The University of North Carolina, Chapel Hill.

Gupta, S. S., Henninger, W. R., & Vinh, M. E. (2014). *First steps to preschool inclusion: How to jumpstart your programwide plan.* Baltimore, MD: Paul H. Brookes Publishing Co.

Horn, E. M., Palmer, S. B., Butera, G. D., & Lieber, J. A. (2016). *Six steps to inclusive preschool curriculum: A UDL-based framework for children's school success.* Baltimore, MD: Paul H. Brookes Publishing Co.

McWilliam, R. A., & Casey, A. M. (2008). *Engagement of every child in the preschool classroom.* Baltimore, MD: Paul H. Brookes Publishing Co.

Odom, S. L. (Ed.). (2001). *Widening the circle: Including children with disabilities in preschool programs.* New York, NY: Teachers College Press.

Odom, S. L., Buysse, V., & Soukakou, E. (2011). Inclusion for young children with disabilities: A quarter century of research perspectives. *Journal of Early Intervention, 33*(4), 344–356.

U.S. Department of Health and Human Services & Department of Education. (2015). *Policy statement on inclusion of children with disabilities in early childhood programs.* Retrieved from https://ed.gov/policy/speced/guid/earlylearning/joint-statement-full-text.pdf

COLLABORATION AND TEAMING

Boyer, V. E., & Thompson, S. D. (2014). Transdisciplinary model and early intervention: Building collaborative relationships. *Young Exceptional Children, 17*(3), 19–32.

Buysse, V., & Wesley, P. W. (2005). *Consultation in early childhood settings.* Baltimore, MD: Paul H. Brookes Publishing Co.

DeVore, S., Miolo, G., & Hader, J. (2011). Individualizing inclusion for preschool children using collaborative consultation. *Young Exceptional Children, 14*(4), 31–43.

Dinnebeil, L. A., & McInerney, W. F. (2011). *A guide to itinerant early childhood special education services.* Baltimore, MD: Paul H. Brookes Publishing Co.

Horn, E., & Jones, H. (Eds.). (2004). *Young Exceptional Children.* [Monograph Series No. 6]. Longmont, CO: Sopris West Educational Services.

King-Sears, M. E., Janney, R., Snell, M. E., Renberg, J., Hamberger, R., Ainsworth, M., . . . Morrison, C. (2015). *Teachers' guides to inclusive practices: Collaborative teaming* (3rd ed.). Baltimore, MD: Paul H. Brookes Publishing Co.

Wesley, P. W. (2002). Early intervention consultation in the classroom: Simple steps for building strong collaboration. *Young Children, 57*(4), 30–34.

CURRICULUM MODIFICATIONS AND EMBEDDED LEARNING OPPORTUNITIES

Campbell, P. H., Kennedy, A. A., & Milbourne, S. A. (2012). *Cara's kit for toddlers: Creating adaptations for routines and activities.* Baltimore, MD: Paul H. Brookes Publishing Co.

Cook, R. E., Klein, M. D., & Chen, D. (2012). *Adapting early childhood curricula for children with special needs* (9th ed.). Boston, MA: Pearson.

Gauvreau, A. (2017). Using "snack talk" to promote social communication in inclusive preschool classrooms. *Young Exceptional Children, 20*(4). doi.org/10.1177/1096250617725503

Horn, E. M., & Banerjee, R. (2009). Understanding curriculum modifications and embedded learning opportunities in the context of supporting all children's success. *Language, Speech, and Hearing Services in Schools, 40,* 406–415.

Kidder, J. E., & McDonnell, A. P. (2017). Visual aids for positive behavior support of young children with autism spectrum disorders. *Young Exceptional Children, 20*(3), 103–116.

Schwartz, I. S., Sandall, S. R., & Gauvreau, A. (2013). Planning to individualize: Meeting the needs of all children using activity matrices. *Teaching Young Children, 7*(2), 21–23.

Snyder, P., Hemmeter, M. L., McLean, M. E., Sandall, S. R., & McLaughlin, T. (2013). Embedded instruction to support early learning in response to intervention frameworks. In V. Buysse & E. S. Peisner-Feinberg (Eds.), *Handbook of response to intervention in early childhood* (pp. 283–298). Baltimore, MD: Paul H. Brookes Publishing Co.

Timler, G. R., Vogler-Elias, D., & McGill, K. F. (2007). Strategies for promoting generalization of social communication skills in preschoolers and school-aged children. *Topics in Language Disorders, 27*(2), 167–181.

INSTRUCTIONAL STRATEGIES

Grisham-Brown, J., & Hemmeter, M. L. (2017). *Blended practices for teaching young children in inclusive settings* (2nd ed.). Baltimore, MD: Paul H. Brookes Publishing Co.

Johnson, J., Rahn, N. L., & Bricker, D. D. (2015). *An activity-based approach to early intervention* (4th ed.). Baltimore, MD: Paul H. Brookes Publishing Company Co.

McBride, B. J., & Schwartz, I. S. (2003). Effects of teaching early interventionists to use discrete trials during ongoing classroom activities. *Topics in Early Childhood Special Education, 23*(1), 5–18.

Schwartz, I. S., Ashmun, J., McBride, B., Scott, C., & Sandall, S. R. (2017). *The DATA model for teaching preschoolers with autism.* Baltimore, MD: Paul H. Brookes Publishing Co.

Snyder, P. A., & Hemmeter, M.L. (2018). *Instruction: Effective strategies to support engagement, learning, and outcomes.* [Monograph Series No. 4]. Washington, DC: Division for Early Childhood.

CLASSROOM-BASED ASSESSMENT

Cook, R. J. (2004). Embedding assessment of young children into routines of inclusive settings: A systematic planning approach. *Young Exceptional Children, 7*(3), 2–11.

Gischlar, K. L., Hojnoski, R. L., & Missall, K. N. (2009). Improving child outcomes with data-based decision making: Interpreting and using data. *Young Exceptional Children, 13,* 2–18.

Hojnoski, R. L., Gischlar, K. L., & Missall, K. N. (2009). Improving child outcomes with data-based decision making: Collecting data. *Young Exceptional Children, 12,* 32–44.

Hojnoski, R. L., Gischlar, K. L., & Missall, K. N. (2009). Improving child outcomes with data-based decision making: Graphing data. *Young Exceptional Children, 12,* 15–30.

McLean, M., Hemmeter, M. L., & Snyder, P. (2014). *Essential elements for assessing infants and preschoolers with special needs.* Upper Saddle River, NJ: Pearson.

INDEPENDENCE

Baker, B. L., & Brightman, A. J. (with Blacher, J.B., Heifetz, L.J., Hinshaw, S.P., & Murphy, D.M.). (2004). *Steps to independence: Teaching everyday skills to children with special needs* (4th ed.). Baltimore, MD: Paul H. Brookes Publishing Co.

Bruns, D. A., & Thompson, S. D. (2012). *Feeding challenges in young children: Strategies and specialized interventions for success.* Baltimore, MD: Paul H. Brookes Publishing Co.

Durand, V. M. (2013). *Sleep better! A guide to improving sleep for children with special needs* (Rev. ed.). Baltimore, MD: Paul H. Brookes Publishing Co.

Suppo, J. L., & Mayton, M. R. (2012). A portable potty plan for children with autism. *Young Exceptional Children, 15*(4), 3–16.

LANGUAGE AND COMMUNICATION

Bardige, B. (2015). *Talk to me, baby: How you can support young children's language development* (2nd ed.). Baltimore, MD: Paul H. Brookes Publishing Co.

Battaglia, D. (2017). Functional communication training in children with autism spectrum disorder. *Young Exceptional Children, 20*(1), 30–40.

Coogle, C. G., Floyd, K., Hanline, M. F., & Kellner-Hiczewski, J. (2013). Strategies used in natural environments to promote communication development in young children at risk for autism spectrum disorder. *Young Exceptional Children, 16*(3), 11–23.

Dickinson, D. K., & Tabors, P. O. (Eds.). (2001). *Beginning literacy with language: Young children learning at home and school.* Baltimore, MD: Paul H. Brookes Publishing Co.

Hart, B., & Risley, T. R. (1995). *Meaningful differences in the everyday experience of young American children.* Baltimore, MD: Paul H Brookes Publishing Co.

LITERACY

Abbott, M., Beecher, C., Petersen, S., Greenwood, C. R., & Atwater, J. (2017). A team approach to data-driven decision-making literacy instruction in preschool classrooms: Child assessment and intervention through classroom team self-reflection. *Young Exceptional Children, 20*(3), 117–132.

Dennis, L. R., & Horn, E. (2011). Strategies for supporting early literacy development. *Young Exceptional Children, 14*(3), 29–40.

Dennis, L. R., Lynch, S. A., & Stockall, N. (2012). Planning literacy environments for diverse preschoolers. *Young Exceptional Children, 15*(3), 3–19.

Ezell, H. K., & Justice, L. M. (2005). *Shared storybook reading: Building young children's language and emergent literacy skills.* Baltimore, MD: Paul H. Brookes Publishing Co.

Fleury, V. P., & Schwartz, I. S. (2017). A modified dialogic reading intervention for preschool children with autism spectrum disorder. *Topics in Early Childhood Special Education, 37*(1), 16–28.

Mihai, A., Friesen, A., Butera, G., Horn, E., Lieber, J., & Palmer, S. (2015). Teaching phonological awareness to all children through storybook reading. *Young Exceptional Children, 18*(4), 3–18.

Shanahan, T., & Lonigan, C. J. (Eds.). (2013). *Early childhood literacy: The National Early Literacy Panel and beyond.* Baltimore, MD: Paul H. Brookes Publishing Co.

MATH AND SCIENCE

Donegan-Ritter, M. (2017). STEM for ALL children: Preschool teachers supporting engagement of children with special needs in physical science learning centers. *Young Exceptional Children, 20*(1), 3–15.

Fuson, K. C., Clements, D. H., & Sarama, J. (2015). Making early math education work for all children. *Phi Delta Kappan, 97*(3), 63–68.

Hintz, A., & Smith, A. T. (2013). Mathematizing read-alouds in three easy steps. *The Reading Teacher, 67*(2), 103–108.

Kuder, B. N., & Hojnoski, R. L. (2018). Under construction: Strategic changes in the block area to promote engagement and learning. *Young Exceptional Children, 21*(2), 76–91.

Moomaw, S., & Davis, A. (2010). STEM comes to preschool. *Young Children, 65*(5), 12–14.

Notari-Syverson, A., & Sadler, F. H. (2008). Math is for everyone: Strategies for supporting early mathematical competencies in young children. *Young Exceptional Children, 11*(3), 2–16.

FRIENDSHIPS AND SOCIAL COMPETENCE

Brown, W. H., Odom, S. L., & McConnell, S. R. (Eds.). (2008). *Social competence of young children: Risk, disability, and intervention.* Baltimore, MD: Paul H. Brookes Publishing Co.

Favazza, P. C., Ostrosky, M. M., & Mouzourou, C. (2016). *The Making Friends program: Supporting acceptance in your K–2 classroom.* Baltimore, MD: Paul H. Brookes Publishing Co.

Hendrix, R., Palmer, K. Z., Tarshis, N., & Winner, M. G. (2013). *The incredible flexible you: A social thinking curriculum for the preschool and early elementary years.* San Jose, CA: Social Thinking.

Joseph, G. E., & Strain, P. S. (2010). Teaching young children interpersonal problem-solving skills. *Young Exceptional Children, 13*(3), 28–40.

Stanton-Chapman, T. L., & Hadden, D. S. (2011). Encouraging peer interactions in preschool classrooms: The role of the teacher. *Young Exceptional Children, 14*(1), 17–28.

CHALLENGING BEHAVIOR

Dunlap, G., Fox, L., Lee, J. K., Strain, P. S., Vatland, C., Joseph, J. D., & Turnbull, A. (2016). *Prevent-Teach-Reinforce for families: A model of individualized positive behavior support for home and community.* Baltimore, MD: Paul H. Brookes Publishing Co.

Dunlap, G., Wilson, K., Strain, P., & Lee, J.K. (2013). *Prevent-Teach-Reinforce for young children.* Baltimore, MD: Paul H. Brookes Publishing Co.

Hemmeter, M. L., Ostrosky, M. M., & Corso, R. M. (2012). Preventing and addressing challenging behavior: Common questions and practical strategies. *Young Exceptional Children, 15*(2), 32–46.

Johnson, L. D., & Monn, E. (2015). Bridging behavioral assessment and behavioral intervention: Finding your inner behavior analyst. *Young Exceptional Children, 18*(3), 19–35.

Ostrosky, M. M., & Sandall, S. R. (Eds.). (2013). *Addressing young children's challenging behaviors. Young Exceptional Children.* [Monograph Series No. 15]. Los Angeles, CA: The Division for Early Childhood of the Council for Exceptional Children.

Powell, D., Dunlap, G., & Fox, L. (2006). Prevention and intervention for the challenging behaviors of toddlers and preschoolers. *Infants & Young Children, 19*(1), 25–35.

Wood, B. K., & Ferro, J. B. (2014). An effective approach to developing function-based interventions in early childhood classrooms. *Young Exceptional Children, 17*(1), 3–20.

ELECTRONIC RESOURCES

ASD Toddler Initiative

https://asdtoddler.fpg.unc.edu/

Autism Focused Intervention Resources & Modules (AFIRM)

https://afirm.fpg.unc.edu

Centers for Disease Control and Prevention: Learn the Signs. Act Early.

www.cdc.gov/ncbddd/actearly

Center on the Social and Emotional Foundations for Early Learning

http://csefel.vanderbilt.edu/

Division for Early Childhood (DEC)

www.dec-sped.org/

Early Childhood Technical Assistance Center

http://ectacenter.org/

Haring Center for Research and Training in Inclusive Education

http://haringcenter.org/

Head Start Center for Inclusion

www.headstartinclusion.org

Head Start/Early Childhood Learning & Knowledge Center

https://eclkc.ohs.acf.hhs.gov/

IRIS Center: Resource Locator

iris.peabody.vanderbilt.edu/resources/iris-resource-locator/ (specifically early childhood modules)

National Association for the Education of Young Children (NAEYC)

www.naeyc.org

National Center for Pyramid Model Innovations (NCPMI)

www.Challengingbehavior.org

Paul H. Brookes Publishing Co. (2017). *Learn & Play Tip a Day* (Version 1.2.0). Baltimore, MD: Author.

https://www.brookespublishing.com/resource-library/learn-play-tip-day-app/ (available on Apple and Android devices)

Swift Education Center

www.swiftschools.org/

The National Professional Development Center on Autism Spectrum Disorder

https://autismpdc.fpg.unc.edu/evidence-based-practices

Universal Design for Learning (UDL) Guidelines

www.udlcenter.org/aboutudl/udlguidelines

University of Washington: Cultivate Learning

https://depts.washington.edu/cqel/

Index

Tables and figures are indicated with *t* and *f*.